The Savage Side

The Savage Side

Reclaiming Violent Models of God

B. JILL CARROLL

ROWMAN & LITTLEFIELD PUBLISHERS, INC.
Lanham • Boulder • New York • Oxford

ROWMAN & LITTLEFIELD PUBLISHERS, INC.

Published in the United States of America
by Rowman & Littlefield Publishers, Inc.
4720 Boston Way, Lanham, Maryland 20706
www.rowmanlittlefield.com

12 Hid's Copse Road
Cumnor Hill, Oxford OX2 9JJ, England

British Library Cataloguing in Publication Information Available

Library of Congress Cataloging-in-Publication Data

Carroll, B. Jill, 1963–
    The savage side: reclaiming violent models of God / B. Jill Carroll.
        p. cm.
    Includes bibliographical references and index.
    ISBN 0-7425-1281-9 (alk. paper)—ISBN 0-7425-1282-7 (pbk. : alk. paper)
    1. Natural theology. 2. God—Attributes. 3. Violence—Religious aspects. I. Title

BL182.c27 2001
211—dc21

2001019880

Printed in the United States of America

♾™ The paper used in this publication meets the minimum requirements of American
National Standard for Information Sciences—Permanence of Paper for Printed Library
Materials, ANSI/NISO Z39.48-1992.

Contents

Acknowledgments

For financial support, I am grateful to the Woodrow Wilson National Fellowship Foundation and the American Academy of Religion. Additionally, I am indebted to: Corie Schweitzer for her technical expertise and her good eye; to the editors at Rowman & Littlefield for being willing to take a chance; to numerous colleagues and students for their helpful insights on this work; to Kathryn Glenney for her unfailing love and encouragement; and finally, to Annie Dillard for her accessibility and graciousness over the last ten years and for her work.

Thank you all.

Chapter 1

Natural Theology or Political Theology?

The work of Rene Girard, Georges Bataille, and others has focused on the place of violence in relation to religion and whatever is considered to be 'the sacred'. Most of this work, however, has been preoccupied with violence as it relates to religious ritual and practice. What receives little or no discussion in these accounts is the place of violence in relation to the deity itself: to God. In much contemporary constructive theology, notions of violence in reference to God have been excised from the discussion because of their incommensurability with certain ideological and political sensibilities—mainly those of some liberation and feminist theologians. The central argument of this book holds that the models of God that have emerged from a dominant strand of contemporary feminist religious thought are reductionistic, utilitarian, and domesticate the concept of 'God'. I propose a new natural theology based on the violence of the natural world as a focus for explicating the being of the divine. The two major thinkers in this critique of feminist models of God are Annie Dillard and Emmanuel Levinas—two figures one would not normally place together in a theological or philosophical discussion because of the disparity of their subject matter, style, and immediate philosophical orientations. Dillard, the Pulitzer Prize-winning author whose nature writing finds its literary heritage in nineteenth- and twentieth-century romanticism and American transcendentalism, is also influenced by Neoplatonism, Whiteheadian process thought, Hasidic Judaism, and quantum physics. Levinas was a Jewish French phenomenologist whose philosophical work after the 1950s focused on a critique of Western ontology as subordinating ethics to the classical themes of being and knowledge. Levinas interprets ethics in relation to the face of the Other—the face being the condition of an ethic that exposes the totalizing tendency of the Cartesian subject. Despite the differences between Dillard and Levinas, which will be elucidated carefully, I argue that their models of God resemble and complement each other and, together, form a critique of the models of God offered by feminist religious thought.

Most feminist theologians in America, convinced that the male, hierarchically dominant Father God of traditional Judeo-Christian thought demands and even causes their subjugation, have drastically altered their conceptions of God in order to further more egalitarian understandings of human/human, human/earth and human/divine relationships. Consequently, anything resembling violence has been removed from models of God and has been replaced exclusively by attributes of benevolence. Violence or savagery as a feature of a model of God is viewed by these feminist theologians as detrimental to women and their struggle for liberation from aspects of traditional Jewish and Christian thought and institutions—specifically those traditions which incorporate the dominant, male, hierarchically superior model of God they find objectionable.

One such feminist theologian is Sallie McFague; her book *Models of God: Theology for an Ecological, Nuclear Age* has received a great deal of attention since its publication in 1987. Many characterize it as the first attempt at a feminist systematic theology, and it serves as the theological backbone of McFague's later work. I see McFague's work as a type of much of the constructive theology done by those with feminist, liberationist, and/or environmentalist sensibilities, not only because the book itself shares these sensibilities, but also because the book has been championed as a groundbreaking work that illustrates the restructuring of thought that needs to take place in order to rid the Western world of its sexism, racism, imperialism, and other oppressive thought patterns and actions. Here, I will use McFague's thought as a prototype of the kind of work being done by many feminist constructive theologians working within Western religious categories, especially those categories that deal with models of God; furthermore, McFague's work serves as an example of the prevalent feminist theological perspective which I will critique and to which I will offer an alternative.

At the risk of being reductionistic, one may say that McFague's thought centers around two broad notions or underlying presuppositions. First, she holds the most basic claim of the Christian faith to be an assertion that "the universe is neither indifferent or malevolent but that there is a power (and a personal power at that) which is on the side of life and its fulfillment" (McFague 1987, x). Second, McFague assumes the "thoroughgoing, radical interdependence of life at all levels in every imaginable way" (x). Words like "relationship," "connection," and "organic" are used quite frequently in McFague's entire discussion and form a sort of verbal front against all that is wrong with traditional models of God and God's relation to the world. In simple terms, she opposes any understanding of God and the God/world relation that is hierarchical, dualistic, unchanging, atomistic, anthropocentric, and deterministic and supports only those that are open, caring, inclusive, interdependent, changing, mutual, and creative (13).

These two broad notions—that the power of the universe is personal and benevolent, and that every living thing is in relation to every other living thing—form the general grid of McFague's thinking as a whole. Into this framework she places her method of doing theology, a method centering on the definition and function of metaphor. She says that "the essence of metaphorical theology is precisely the refusal to identify human constructions with divine reality" (McFague 1987, 22). She operates on the assumption of the *via negativa*, which sees God as irreducible to language, and in her words, "all language about God misses the mark" (23). Theologians, therefore, are afforded great freedom in talking about God as long as the models decided upon speak to the sensibilities of the current situation, not one of a past era in history. McFague focuses on the 'is' and 'is not' character of metaphor and tries to walk a line between seeing theology as a verbal game, as she claims deconstructionists do, and as seeing no role whatsoever for the imagination in theology, as do fundamentalists and literalists.

In light of these parameters and assumptions, McFague proposes four primary models of God and the God/world relation: God as mother, lover, and friend and the earth as God's body. In her book she discusses each model in detail, focusing on the type of actions and attitudes each model encourages on the part of humans, as well as what each models illumines about God. I will focus my attention here on McFague's model of the earth as God's body, mainly because I see the other three models as derivative of her primary understanding of the God/nature relation and because it is this very relation with which I am most concerned.

The two sides of the metaphor of 'the earth as God's body' are, quite obviously, the earth and God, and these two are placed into relation in McFague's thinking so that the earth reflects God in a substantial way. God's relation to the earth is such that "all phenomena in reality have the potential for reflecting the deity" (McFague 1987, 135). This is a type of broad sacramentality in which God and the world are seen not as synonymous with each other, as in pantheism, but as reflective of each other's will and nature; they reflect each other's personality, to speak anthropomorphically and in keeping with metaphorical theology. God is, then, intimately connected to a world that is like her and reflects her nature and likeness; it has her features even in its freedom.

McFague's aligning of God and nature is not a problem in my view; however, a significant problem that I see with McFague's models is that the models of God as mother, lover, and friend—and any other such "warm, fuzzy" models—do not square with the model of the earth as God's body if one is honest about the terrifying and threatening aspects of the natural world. McFague romanticizes the natural world, avoiding the violence contained therein, in order to support her assumption that the power of the universe is benevolent and is, therefore, concerned about and identified with certain political and social struggles, namely those of feminists, liberationists, and environmentalists. She insists on benevolent, non-violent models of God in spite of the fact that the world that supposedly reflects this nice God casts quite a different image than the mother/lover/friend she envisions. She takes the wildly complex and disturbing models of God that a close aligning of God and nature produces, and either ignores them, domesticates them in order not to offend the current human comfort zone, or both. My account of natural theology shares a common conviction underlying the work of feminists such as Sallie McFague and that of Dillard: God, or the divine, is in close proximity to the natural world. But my conception of nature, rooted in Dillard, differs radically from that of McFague and others like her. Dillard's goal is "to loose the methods of literary criticism upon the raw world . . . to consider the raw world as a text, as a meaningful, purposefully fashioned creation, as a work of art" (Dillard 1982a, 144). By "raw world" she means primarily nature, and in *Pilgrim at Tinker Creek* she analyzes the raw, natural world in order to determine what kind of power shapes it and is reflected in it; she calls this power, this artist, "God." The model of God that I propose and that emerges from *Pilgrim* and other books by Dillard, diverges from the soothing models explicated in McFague's (and others') work. Dillard's God is a God of exuberant beauty and grace *as well as* a God of "crazed" extravagance, "lunatic" design, and a God who is not so thin-skinned as to wince at the death of his creations—even the human ones. McFague's God, on the other hand, bolstered by metaphors of God as mother, lover, and friend and the earth as God's body, stems from a highly romanticized view of nature that ignores the aspects of the natural universe that would disrupt such comforting models and metaphors of God. I argue that if nature is to be seen as in any way representative of deity, which I mean to affirm, then the beautiful *and* the horrifying aspects of nature are to be considered in constructing the doctrine of God; therefore, I favor the Dillardian view for its unflinching honesty and its superior reading of the text of nature, the "raw data" of the universe.

Levinas, coming from an intellectual horizon in sharp contrast to Dillard's, in *Totality and Infinity* articulates the asymmetrical (non-)relation between the face of the Other and the I of Cartesian subjectivity and rationality. The Other comes from "beyond the horizon" and calls into question the self-sufficiency of the I, and exposes the violence done by the I to the Other in totalizing activities of cognition, production and appropriation. In such activities, the radical alterity (otherness) of the Other becomes a content of consciousness, or, as Levinas says, is reduced to an "economy of the same." The Other's face appears as if from beyond in an "epiphanic trace," and Levinas casts this trace in the third person as "illeity," which is the place of God in Levinas's account. Chief among Levinas's concerns is to conceive of an ethical subjectivity that would avoid the violence of Western ontology (Levinas 1969).

Another line of inquiry, however, is to ask what violence *remains* in Levinas's account of the asymmetrical relation between the Other and the I. I demonstrate that there are two levels of violence. First, there is the violence committed by the I against the Other, which I argue has been committed by feminist theologians against deity by domesticating deity. Next, there is the violence that the Other does to the I, the violence that is indicative of the rupture of the domesticating, reductionistic categories of thought placed upon the Other when the Other is regarded as an object of utility, in that the Other is conceived of only in terms accommodating to political, ideological sensibilities. Finally, I argue that despite Levinas's stress on persons rather than nature, nature can be cast as an Other in Levinas's structure so that the threads of connection on this issue between Levinas and Dillard are illumined.

Dillard and Levinas serve as the primary textual loci for this book. I also allude to selections of the work of Jacques Derrida, Ludwig Feuerbach, Sigmund Freud, and Friedrich Nietzsche. Derrida has certain affinities with Levinas inasmuch as he defines deconstruction as, among other things, an openness to radical alterity and whatever has been repressed or marginalized for the sake of cognition, easy representation, the Good, or the True. Deconstruction, as an ethical technique, is aware that "representation conceals, while pretending to reveal, the seething turbulence, the radical otherness of being" (Wyschogrod 1989, 191). This "seething turbulence" may serve as a trope for the aspects of a model of God, a turbulence that many are tempted to moderate because of convenience or expediency. Older critiques of religion offered by Feuerbach and Freud are relevant in that they locate the impetus for religion and belief in God in human desire, projection, and wish fulfillment. These are powerful critiques that I plan to levy against feminist models of God. Furthermore, I argue that Dillardian models may survive, in important respects, the Feuerbachian/Freudian critiques in that they have very little affinity with the benevolent models at which Feuerbach's and Freud's critiques are aimed. Finally, I focus upon Nietzsche's critique of religious and philosophical systems that refuse to acknowledge and affirm the tragic aspects of existence. I suggest that a sense of the tragic is conspicuously absent in dominant feminist thought, but that, conversely, Dillard's religious vision builds upon the reality of the tragic.

Traditionally, nature is used by theologians to prove the existence of God or, by Christian apologists, to demonstrate the means of salvation for those who live and die without knowledge of Christ. My interest in nature as a ground for theology bypasses such concerns entirely. I am concerned with the givenness of nature in all its beauty and horror, its perpetual elusiveness and otherness, and its ultimate resistance to domestication; moreover, I use these aspects of nature as loci for religious meaning. In addition, I contend that the hierarchical and violent models of God that seem to have dominated the Western religious tradition cannot be reduced to patriarchal ideology and interests. This is not to say that patriarchal interests, or any other interests or agendas for that matter, have no role in constructing models of God. Feminist thought for over two decades has illustrated amply and convincingly the ways in which certain conceptions of God—reified and canonized by sacred texts, rituals, liturgies, etc.—further the interests of sexism, various colonizations, and exploitation. I do not agree, however, that patriarchal interests account completely for the rise and continued prominence of models of God that emphasize violence and domination. Such models exist, at least partially, because of the human experience of power*less*ness in the face of the power*ful*ness of the natural world. Humans everywhere and in all known times have experienced or witnessed, albeit within varying cultural, social, economic, and gendered contexts, the destructive and savage side of the natural world. In the face of such power, human material accomplishments often find their end in piles of twisted steel and broken concrete. Furthermore, the wonderfully thoughtful, expressive, and vibrant people who swirl and dance the human drama along century after century find their bodies thrown and maimed, their lives abruptly ended in the blink of an eye by gusting winds of hurricanes, the crazed strength of tornados, the drowning waves of lava or tides or rains, the steady gnaw of viruses, or by some other severe, seemingly merciless and hostile agent of the natural world. The violence of the natural world toward humanity and the human powerlessness that is revealed in the face of such violence are the grounds, at least partially, for conceptions of God that emphasize the deity's domination and hierarchical superiority. To reduce such conceptions to ideological interests, such as those of patriarchy, is simplistic and ignores a significant aspect of human experience. The prevailing feminist analyses of models of deity based on violence and domination are important and ring true in many respects; however, such an analysis is only one of many ways these models can be read. Furthermore, additional analyses and appropriations of these models can exist alongside the feminist critiques of them without undercutting their validity entirely. It is my hope that those models that have been cast aside can be rehabilitated by reading them through a new hermeneutical grid grounded in an understanding of nature's ferocity, and that the vast range of human experience from which they derive can be represented more truly.

Nature and Theology: American Transcendentalism

Since 1975, when she won the Pulitzer Prize for general nonfiction for her book *Pilgrim at Tinker Creek*, Annie Dillard has become one of the most revered contemporary nature writers and is named often as an almost direct literary descendant of Henry David Thoreau. The link between Dillard and nineteenth century American transcendentalism is an important one; however, most treatments of this linkage focus almost exclusively on the literary similarities between Dillard and her transcendentalist predecessors. What receives scant attention in various studies of Dillard's work are the appropriations she makes from the theological and philosophical milieu of nineteenth century American transcendentalism which, in turn, gleaned ideas from not only its own immediate past and present, but from antiquity. The philosophical and theological premise of Dillard's nature writing is found primarily in the Neoplatonism of American transcendentalism, specifically its Emersonian version, and in the Calvinist sacramentality characteristic of the theology of the Puritans. These two important aspects of Dillard's intellectual heritage deserve discussion here in order to draw into sharper relief Dillardian conceptions of deity, which will be dealt with later.

Scholars who study transcendentalism have documented the important role Platonism played in the transcendentalist movement, especially in the thought of its leader, Ralph Waldo Emerson.[1] Platonism was the philosophical tool Emerson used to reject the eighteenth century epistemology and view of nature, and to assert his own theory of the correspondence between the spiritual and the natural worlds. From his Unitarian ancestors, Emerson was bequeathed an epistemology fashioned according to the rationalism of Locke and the Scottish common-sense philosophy of Thomas Reid and his followers. From this rationalism, combined with Newtonian scientific theory, emerged a view of Reason and of human relation with nature that Emerson found objectionable.

One of the aims of John Locke's *Essay Concerning Human Understanding* is to refute those about him in seventeenth century England who adhered to the notion of innate truth. The doctrine of innate truths is the answer Platonic philosophy gave to the question of the origin of true knowledge. According to Plato, ideas must be innate in the mind, or else one would not be able to recognize true knowledge when confronted with it. In *Meno*, Plato has Socrates explain that because the soul is immortal "and has been born many times, and has seen both the things here on earth and those in the underworld and all things, there is nothing that it has not learned" (Plato 1985, 65). Therefore, "the whole of searching and learning is recollection" (67). Innate ideas remain latent in the mind until life experience retrieves them from their dormant state and they become fully revealed. Learning is, then, "a process of reminiscence" (Jeffreys 1967, 44). For Plato, gaining knowledge was primarily a mental activity and secondarily a matter of experience or the senses. It is this aspect of the Platonic epistemology that Locke repudiates in his *Essay*. Locke, an architect of empiricism, reverses the Platonic priority of the mind over the senses and argued that knowledge comes through sensory experience. The mind, rather than being the depository for innate ideas, is a *tabula rasa* on which sensory impressions are made. Locke argues that were ideas innate in the mind, they would be held universally by all people. As he explains in the *Essay*, such universal assent is not maintained because there are those, e.g., children, who seem to be exempted from this assent. Even if universal assent could be shown, Locke argues that it would not necessarily prove that ideas were innate; there could be another account of their universality (Book I, Ch. 2, sec. 1–5). It is observation of the world (both external and internal), not reminiscence, that accounts for the growth of the mind and the attainment of knowledge (Jeffreys, 46–7). In refuting the belief in innate ideas, Locke rejects also the Platonic idea on which the notion of innate ideas rests—of correspondence between the realm of the mind and the eternal, pure realm of the forms. It is this aspect of the Platonic system that becomes central in the thought of Emerson and other American transcendentalists, and will be discussed later.

Locke's theory of knowledge based on sense experience shows the impact of Newtonian science, which by the eighteenth century had influenced conceptions of the human/nature relationship as well. Nature, in the eighteenth-century scientific worldview, was the stable ground on which the observer of empirical phenomena could stand in order to inductively ascertain the mechanical laws of the universe. Nature, unlike history or society, was not man-made and, thus, offered a measure of epistemological stability and clarity (Cherry 1980, 3). This apparent stability, however, crumbled under the critiques of Hume and Kant, and "as the eighteenth century passed into the nineteenth, 'nature' was in definitional disarray and its previously assumed stability under question" (Cherry, 5). It is from within the middle of this disarray that Emerson emerges to repudiate the scientific outlook for its cold and barren theories of knowledge (Locke), and for the ease with which nature was dismissed as a ground for true knowledge.[2] By retrieving a version of Platonism via his own readings of Plotinus and Proclus and the teaching he received from British philosopher Thomas Taylor, and by asserting the truth of Sampson Reed's theory on the growth of the mind over against the Lockian perspective, Emerson was able to proffer a vision of human existence in the world that relied upon: correspondence between the spiritual and material worlds, emotion and perception as vital aspects of Reason, and nature as the mediator between God and humans as well as central to the growth of the human mind.

That Emerson's theory of correspondence between the spiritual and natural worlds finds its origin in Platonic and Neoplatonic thought is widely attested. Emerson received his training in this vein not only from his own readings of primary Platonic sources, evidenced by notes in his journals on his readings of Plotinus and Proclus (Brown 1945, 335–36), but also "with the aid of Thomas Taylor, a British scholar who gave his readings a Neoplatonic and mystical cast" (Albanese 1988, 1120; Paul 1965, 28). Emerson's theory of correspondence relies most specifically on the Plotinian theory of emanation, emanation being the means by which all things derive from the One and exist in hierarchical relation to the One. The world proceeds from the One, the intelligible God, and exists in a hierarchy of being which "extends from the gods who impart life to the stars down to inorganic matter through the daemons, the virtuous souls, the rational beings, the animals, and the plants. There is no being which is not living, even those which in appearance are lifeless" (Brehier 1958, 165). As Armstrong explains, "the lower hypostases are produced by a spontaneous and necessary efflux of life or power from the One, which leaves their source in itself undiminished" (Armstrong 1979, 61). The philosophical subtleties of this theory in its Plotinian context and the later debates over the proper Plotinian relation to matter need not concern us here. Neither did they concern Emerson; he appropriated, in an opportunistic fashion, from these ancients and their "past speculation about the nature of man and the universe any idea that pointed in the direction of their correspondence" (Paul 1965, 28). For Emerson, the goal was to find a way to join the two halves of reality: the spiritual and the material or natural. The Neoplatonic idea of emanation served this goal, in Emerson's view, by having the material world be a direct product—an emanation—from the spiritual realm, so that the two are not opposed to each other, but are inextricably intertwined and reflective of each other. Neoplatonism, as Emerson understood it, provided philosophical support for the idea "that the spiritual and natural universes share the same law, that although the natural is an imitation and therefore inferior world, its analogical identity with the Creator and the spiritual universe gives it (and the man who lives in it) a spiritual significance" (Paul, 3–4). So, for Emerson, the natural world is not simply an object of experience or an appearance rather than the thing itself (Kant), nor is its order simply due to the imposition of belief (Hume) (Cherry 1980, 4–5). Nature, by virtue of being an extension of the Creator, has spiritual import and can serve as an epistemological ground for ultimate truth. Furthermore, nature is important for the development of the mind, an idea Emerson gleaned from Sampson Reed's book *Observations on the Growth of the Mind.*[3]

Emerson read Reed's book shortly after it was published in 1826 and, in letters to friends, ranked it among the works of Plato for its truth and vision. Reed, a young Swedenborgian who owned an apothecary, expounded upon two major ideas which Emerson deemed central to his own project and work: the development of the mind from an internal force, and nature as an important impetus to the growth of the mind (soul) (Reed 1970, v–vii). Early in his book, Reed speaks of "an erroneous sentiment, that the mind is originally vacant, and requires only to be filled up" (Reed, 22). Of course, he is speaking of Locke's theory of learning and knowledge. Against Locke he argues that the "mind is originally a most delicate germ, whose husk is the body; planted in this world, that the light and heat of heaven may fall upon it with a gentle radiance, and call forth its energies" (22). Reed goes on to explain that while outside experience certainly aids the mind in its growth, what must be remembered above all is that the mind grows "not from external accretion, but from an internal principle" (31). So, while Reed does not explicitly (at least in these passages) call for the Platonic doctrine of innate ideas, he makes a similar gesture by placing the impetus for the growth of the mind *within* the mind itself, not outside in the sensory or empirical world. It is not surprising, then, that Emerson would find Reed's theory useful in his own refutation of Locke's epistemology.

For Reed, however, nature remains central to the development of the mind even though the primary force or 'germ' of that development is internal to the mind. "The natural world," he claims, "was precisely and perfectly adapted to invigorate and strengthen the intellectual and moral man" (Reed 1970, 36). His Swedenborgianism (and, by extension, his Neoplatonism) betray themselves most explicitly when he claims that the highest purpose of nature is not to support the various life forms that live within it, but "to draw forth and mature the latent energies of the soul . . . to initiate them into its own mysteries; and by its silent and humble dependence on its Creator, to leave on them . . . the full impression of his likeness" (37). Here, then, over against Locke's notion of the mind as *tabula rasa*, Reed reasserts a version of the Neoplatonic theory of innate ideas; furthermore, against the scientific view of nature as useful only for understanding the mechanical laws of the universe in order to further human purposes, Reed rehabilitates nature as a source not only of the mind's primary development, but also as the ground for spiritual truths. Clearly, as Emerson himself acknowledged, he found a kindred spirit in Reed. Reed even goes on to theorize about the role of the poet in gaining knowledge. The poet, more than anyone else, is to feel and be governed by the spirit of God in creation, and is to pass on "the spark which passes from God to nature" (46). Poetic vision is the "the soul of science," for without poetry science is a "heartless study, distrusting even the presence and power of Him to whom it owes its existence" (43). True poetry, that which becomes immortal, is that "which presents the image of God which is stamped on nature" (43). For Reed and Emerson, therefore, intellect and intuition are wedded; poetic imagination and perception are integral aspects of reason, not simply emotive sentiments that must be discarded when the 'real' work of science or reasoning begins.[4]

Platonic theory appropriated from Neoplatonists like Plotinus and Thomas Taylor, from Swedenborgians such as Reed, and from a pastiche of other minor sources, served Emerson in his quest to solve the problem of maintaining "a living connection between the horizontal-worldly and the vertical-otherworldly . . . to inform the life of the horizontal with the quality of the vertical" (Paul 1965, 25). As Sherman Paul states:

> He needed those elements which the eighteenth century had discarded, which current academic training in Lockean and Scottish common-sense philosophy minimized: a universe of levels, rising to the summit of the spiritual and Real; an account of perception, restoring an intuitive, imaginative faculty of Reason; and a theory of the relation of language to nature, making possible, as the role of the poet, the expression of the Real in the concrete objects of everyday experience. (Paul 1965, 28–9)

With the theory of correspondence in hand, Emerson immersed himself in the natural world, "searching for the analogies between its phenomena and his [God's] thoughts," convinced that it illumined the divine essence (Paul, 30). No longer using nature as merely a field from which to unearth scientific facts, Emerson presupposed that nature, being the mediator between the human and the divine, revealed the character of God more than any book or dogma ever could.

These characteristically Emersonian convictions about the God/nature relationship are important aspects of the philosophical and theological premises of Annie Dillard's work. It is no accident that, when asked to recommend her favorite books, she suggested Emerson's *Essays* and identified her approach to spirituality as one "in the Neoplatonic tradition" (Fitzgerald 1985, 80).[5] Her approach to nature as "raw data" which explicates divine things is indebted to American transcendentalism which, in turn, is heavily informed by Platonic theory. As will be shown later, however, the vision of God that Dillard sees emerging from nature is in sharp opposition to Emerson's vision and to that of other transcendentalists.

Her conception of God is informed, at least partially, by another strand of religious thought that, at first glance, may appear antithetical to the Emersonian vision, but actually forms an integral part of a religious worldview of which transcendentalism is an heir: Puritan Calvinism, its doctrine of God, and its view of the relation between God and nature.

Sherman Paul suggests that even though Emerson received his idea of the correspondence between the spiritual and the material from his readings in Platonism and from continental mystics like Boehme and Swedenborg, he could just as well have "stayed at home" and gotten it from the Puritan, Calvinist theology of Jonathan Edwards (Paul 1965, 3). Edwards, in his *Images or Shadows of Divine Things*, speaks of the material and inferior being a shadow, or bearing a resemblance to, the spiritual. He claims that "the works of nature are intended and contrived of God to signify and indigitate spiritual things" (Edwards 1948, 60, sec. 55).[6] Moreover, he states that "it is very fit and becoming of God . . . so to order things that there should be a voice of His in His works [nature], instructing those that behold them and painting forth and shewing divine mysteries and things more immediately appertaining to Himself and His spiritual kingdom" (61, sec. 57). Edwards's view of the natural world as a type of the spiritual is given a mystical or pantheistic twist, however, in his *Dissertation Concerning the End for which God Created the World*. Perry Miller explains how Edwards, in this treatise, argues that God did not create the world merely to demonstrate his power or to draw glory unto himself; God created the world "out of Himself by a diffusion of Himself into time and space . . . by taking upon Himself the forms of stones and trees and of man . . . for the pure joy of self-expression" (194). By using words such as 'effusion' and 'emanation', Edwards exhibits a mystical, neoplatonist strain in his thinking which, as Conrad Cherry points out, "seems not in sync with the Calvinist view of the gulf between creator and created" (51).[2] Such mysticism represents, however, a Calvinist sacramentality regarding the natural world that the New England Puritans retained even though their British forebears had minimalized "the sense appeal of the sacraments and stressed their didactic function" (Cherry 1980, 23). This sacramentality affords Edwards the opportunity to see imagination, especially the religious imagination, as "the creative, symbol-producing, symbol-detecting power of the mind," especially as it regards nature (Cherry, 8).

So, one can see how Emerson might well have gained what he needed by way of correspondence theory from the theology of Edwards, with which he shares a common background in the Puritans. Catherine Albanese explains that "the Transcendentalists were children of the Puritans, who had early exhibited a mystical strain and an ability to find God in nature . . . [they] were sensitive to the God who was immanent as well as transcendent" (Albanese 1988, 1118). This is not to say that the thought of Edwards and Emerson is the same, but simply to assert that both visions of the relation between the divine and nature make room for a correspondence or analogy between the two, and do not place God and nature in utter opposition to one another. Miller argues this when he claims that

> What is persistent, from the covenant theology . . . to Edwards and to Emerson is
> the Puritan's effort to confront, face to face, the images of a blinding divinity in
> the physical universe, and to look upon that universe without the intermediacy of
> ritual, of ceremony, of the Mass and the confessional. (Miller 1964, 185)

Miller goes on to suggest that Emerson might be defined as "an Edwards in whom the concept of original sin has evaporated" (185). This statement illumines the contrast not only between the two specific men, but also between the perspectives they represent. Not only is a notion of original sin largely absent in Emerson, so is the Edwardian idea of the sovereignty of God, which has its roots in the thought of John Calvin, at least for Edwards. The doctrine of divine sovereignty makes its way into Dillard's work and distinguishes her, in part, from Emersonian transcendentalism. Her version of divine sovereignty, however, is not connected to themes of original sin, predestination, and election as are those of Calvin and Edwards. Rather than indicating a divine ordering of all things into a perfect plan, or an election of some to be saved and some to be damned, or even a plan of salvation, the models of a sovereign God that emerge in Dillard's work, as will be shown later, serve centrally to illumine in the most graphic way possible what James Gustafson calls the "theocentric" quality of the universe. Dillard's models reflect the conviction that the world operates under the influence of forces that do not have exclusively human concerns in mind, forces that often seem willing to disregard human concerns entirely in favor of evolution, death, some other natural process, or simply an interest entirely mysterious to us. Without concerning herself with issues of election, predestination and infant damnation, Dillard joins Edwards in placing herself within a Calvinist heritage that, in the words of Clyde Holbrook, upholds a belief in "the sovereign God who still holds sway over nature, history, and individual men" (Holbrook 1953, 395). Of course, for Dillard, this God who holds sway over nature is demonstrated most clearly *in* and *as* nature, so that it is God via nature who holds sway. Despite the priority Dillard gives to nature in her philosophizing about God, in contrast to Edwards who prioritizes Scripture over nature, their work can be characterized in similar ways. Holbrook says of Edwards:

> Indeed for his own day and ours, original sin, infant damnation, and divine
> sovereignty had become too strong a dose for those whose personal security rested
> in the ordered amiability of the natural world, the innate virtue of men, and the
> tender rational benevolence of a loving heavenly Father. The Northampton pastor
> and theologian played traitor to the emerging American dream of self-sufficiency,
> self-reliance, and that peculiar utilitarianism which conceives God as a convenient
> tool for the self-perfection of Western man. (Holbrook 1953, 386)

I maintain that Dillard's conception of God, like that of Edwards, explodes notions of the "amiability of the natural world" and human self-sufficiency in the face of nature. Dillard's God does not exhibit "the tender rational benevolence of a loving heavenly Father" and, furthermore, is not to be roped like cattle into serving the political, economic, and social goals of the various political theologies that reign in American religious thought today. Dillard, like Edwards, will offend those who think "that religion is best conceived in intra-human terms with God tamed to the point where he can or will execute nothing which would offend a cultured Westerner" (Holbrook, 388). Both Edwards and Dillard are obsessed with "a holy God whose purposes are not identifiable with ours" (Holbrook, 388), and this God which, for Dillard, is seen in and is almost synonymous with nature, contrasts sharply with the God proposed by McFague and other liberation thinkers, a God who can be trusted to share their political convictions and give strength to their activism.[8]

A key difference, however, between Dillard and Edwards (or between Dillard and any philosopher or theologian) is one of methodology. While Dillard's work is informed by a variety of rich philosophical and theological traditions (and contemporary science even more), she is not a philosopher or theologian primarily; she is an artist. Therefore, she appropriates these various traditions as they suit her aesthetic sense, or seem right to her. When she proposes "to loose the methods of literary criticism upon the raw world . . . to consider the raw world as a text" (Dillard 1982a, 144), she identifies herself first as a reader, then as an artist who tries to write what she has read. In reading and writing, she appropriates strands and themes from various traditions, some of which conflict with one another, and uses them as cognitive tools to help in understanding and articulating her vision of the natural world. Definite connections exist between some of the traditions she uses, for example, between Neoplatonism and transcendentalism, or transcendentalism and Calvinism, as I have shown. Differences and distinctions exist between them as well, however, which tend to blur in the hands of the artist, whose aesthetic concerns rank as highly as the philosophical ones. Therefore, Dillard's philosophical or theological method may appear differently at various moments in her work. Some passages may ring more Heraclitian than Emersonian, more Whiteheadian than Platonic; others may bear the marks of *via negativa* and ascetic mysticism. The fact is that *all* these are present in her work to the extent that their perspective supports her endeavor to read the raw, natural world as a text and determine what, if anything, can be said about deity, or the powers that "brood and light" in the universe, powers over which people have little or no control. Furthermore, Dillard has an advantage over her transcendentalist and Calvinist ancestors in that contemporary science affords her a clearer, more dizzying and magnificent vision of the natural world that serves as the "text" for theology. In the next chapter, we begin to see exactly what kind of deity emerges when the natural world—as Dillard understands it—is used as a model or "text" to tell us about God.

Notes

1. See, for example, Stuart Gregory Brown, "Emerson's Platonism," *The New England Quarterly* 18 (September 1945): 325–45; Catherine Albanese, *Corresponding Motion: Transcendental Religion and the New America* (Philadelphia: Temple University Press, 1977) and *Nature Religion in America: From the Algonkian Indians to the New Age* (Chicago: University of Chicago Press, 1990); Sherman Paul, *Emerson's Angle of Vision: Man and Nature in American Experience* (Cambridge: Harvard University Press, 1965); Arnold Smithline, *Natural Religion in American Literature* (New Haven, Conn.: College and University Press, 1966); Conrad Cherry, *Nature and Religious Imagination: From Edwards to Bushnell* (Philadelphia: Fortress Press, 1980); and Philip F. Gura, *The Wisdom of Words: Language, Theology and Literature in the New England Renaissance* (Middletown, Conn.: Wesleyan University Press, 1981).

2. Cherry notes that the eighteenth-century view of nature as a stable and clear epistemological ground was not lost on Emerson even though he rejects the Lockianism entangled with it. According to Cherry, "Emerson would repudiate the scientific outlook in favor of 'Reason' and poetic imagination, but his central word 'nature' had already been baptized and sanctified by previous generations, and his counsel that one should take his personal bearings from the spirit in nature rather than from the opinions in history had the ring of eighteenth century rhetoric" (Cherry 1980, 4).

3. For additional comments on Reed's influence on Emerson, see Philip F. Gura, *The Wisdom of Words: Language, Theology and Literature in the New England Renaissance* (Middletown, Conn.: Wesleyan University Press, 1981): 84–85.

4. Smithline notes that the transcendentalists differed from the rationalists and deists not so much in their conceptions of God, or humanity in relation to God, or on their views of the universe and natural law, but primarily in their view of Reason. He claims this is a difference in method, not conviction (Smithline 1996, 94). Paul argues, however, that Emerson's theory of symbol-using "in which 'the near explains the far" is a shift away from the deist view of nature "as a mechanism from which God was estranged" (Paul 1965, 32–33).

5. "The Good Books: Writer's Choices" by Karen Fitzgerald, *Ms. Magazine* (December 1985), 80. Dillard's other choices were *Waiting for God* by Simone Weil, Martin Buber's *Tales of the Hasidim*, and anything by Abraham Heschel.

6. See also p. 44, sections 7 and 8; p. 56, section 45; p. 65, section 59.

7. Cherry claims that Edwards never really resolves the tension in his thought between pantheism and Calvinistic theism, although both he and Miller acknowledge that Edwards tried to maintain the distinction between God and nature in his thought.

8. Dillard's latent Calvinism is seen not only in her views of deity and sovereignty, but also in what Albanese calls "the Puritan brooding over evil" (170) in her book *Nature Religion in America*. She argues that Dillard shares with the Puritans a perspective in which nature is seen as an "accomplice to what we read as evil, malignant itself" (170). Dillard does not speak of demons and ghosts, as did the Puritans, but she is as sensitive as her forbears to "a negative power, almost a negative sacred, within the natural world" (170).

Chapter 2

God in *Pilgrim at Tinker Creek*

In this chapter, I offer a reading of Dillard's book *Pilgrim at Tinker Creek*, focusing almost exclusively on the image of God that appears in the text, and the contrast between it and that of McFague, inasmuch as McFague's models of God can be seen as typical of those of contemporary American feminist theology, and of contemporary political theology in general.

Mary Cantwell says that, in *Pilgrim at Tinker Creek*, Dillard does this:

> First she guides the reader through the microscope that is her eyes, enlarging frogs, bugs, spiders, water snakes—whatever flies, swims or crawls—to monstrous proportions. Then she aims that microscope, only by now it is a telescope, at the heavens. To perceive God's creatures is, in a sense, to perceive God. (36)

Indeed, a microscope is always close by for Dillard, at least in *Pilgrim*. She says that looking through it is "a moral exercise" and that "the microscope at my forehead is a kind of phylactery, a constant reminder of the facts of creation that I would just as soon forget" (121). Looking at rotifers, amoebas, various worms, blood cells and dozens of other minutae in the natural world not only helps her "discover at least *where* it is that we have been so startlingly set down, if we can't learn why" (12). These forays into the microscopic world help her to characterize the exuberant power that created the world. Nature is God's book, for Dillard, and "you see what kind of Creator it is by looking at the creation" (Moritz 1983, 114). In Stan Goldman's words, "[for Dillard] nature is God's language, and the natural and the supernatural are connected. Thus a walk in the woods of the Blue Ridge Mountains becomes going to church" (198). Or, as Peter Fritzell puts it, "on the banks of Tinker Creek field guide and catechism are about as close as they can be" (219).

This, then, is Dillard's version of Emerson's theory of correspondence rooted, as shown previously, in a Neoplatonic understanding of the relation between nature and the divine. Dillard's understanding of the divine/nature relationship, however, has also been characterized as a panentheistic one, a perspective which "views the natural world as contained within God but sees God as extending beyond the natural world" (Smith, 17). Thus, a mediating position is maintained between pantheism, in which God is synonymous with the natural world, and a theism that would envision God as separated or distinct from, or even opposed to the natural world.[1] Important to note is that Dillard uses the word "God" sparingly in her work, more often using nouns like "creator," "power," "divinity," or "spirit" to speak of that to which the term "God" usually refers. The Dillardian perspective on God can accommodate several approaches to deity, ranging from those which see God as a distinct being to those which use the term "God" to refer to some sort of ground of being or the ultimate power in the universe. I use the term "God" in this work realizing its many possible referents, its polysemic character.

Who, then, is this God that is to be seen in nature? What is s/he like, according to Dillard? Readers get important clues to the answers to these questions early in the opening chapter of *Pilgrim*. The chapter begins:

> I used to have a cat, an old fighting tom, who would jump through an open window by my bed in the middle of the night and land on my chest. I'd half-awaken. He'd stick his skull under my nose and purr, stinking of urine and blood. Some nights he kneaded my bare chest with his front paws, powerfully, arching his back, as if sharpening his claws, or pummeling a mother for milk. And some mornings I'd wake in daylight to find my body covered with paw prints in blood; I looked as though I'd been painted with roses. (1)

She goes on:

> What blood was this, and what roses? It could have been the rose of union, the blood of murder, or the rose of beauty bare and the blood of some unspeakable sacrifice or birth. The sign on my body could have been an emblem or a stain, the keys to the kingdom or the mark of Cain . . . I never knew as I washed, and the blood streaked, faded, and finally disappeared, whether I'd purified myself or ruined the blood sign of the passover. We wake, if we ever wake at all, to mystery, rumors of death, beauty, violence. . . ." (1–2)

While the tomcat is gone and her life has changed, Dillard remembers him as "something powerful playing over me" (2). In the trope of the tomcat, we as readers get our first glimpse of the God that is intimately connected to the mystery, death, beauty and violence of the natural world. God is something powerful that comes abruptly, something that pummels her or sharpens claws on her, something beautiful, mysterious and violent. This passive stance Dillard (and/or the narrator/pilgrim) takes in regard to whatever is the trope for the divine, in this case the tomcat, is maintained throughout the book, for a central part of Dillard's methodology in deriving structures or tropes for God from the natural world, in addition to simply *seeing* things, is to wait passively for them, to let their effects imprint upon her, to let them have their way with her. Such passivity is hinted at again at the end of the first chapter. Dillard has told readers she plans to "explore the neighborhood" around Tinker Creek (11). She has determined that "[w]e don't know what's going on here" in this world that contains within it possibilities for aching beauty as well as cruelty and horror (8). She says:

> We don't know. Our life is a faint tracing on the surface of mystery, like the idle, curved tunnels of leaf miners on the face of a leaf. We must somehow take a wider view, look at the whole landscape, really see it, and describe what's going on here. Then we can at least wail the right question into the swaddling band of darkness, or, if it comes to that, choir the proper praise. (9)

In her effort to "describe what's going on here," she says she is like the arrows certain Indians used to track game they had wounded. The arrows had "lightning marks" on them, carved grooves that channelled the blood from the wound onto the ground so the tracker could find the wounded animal. Dillard says of herself and her book, "I am the arrow shaft, carved along my length by unexpected lights and gashes from the very sky, and this book is the straying trail of blood" (12). Again, she is passive—even as she actively tries to "really see" the world—carved by some power in the sky. What power? In the next sentence she says, "Something pummels us, something barely sheathed. Power broods and lights. We're played on like a pipe; our breath is not our own" (13). The word "pummels" frames the chapter, for it used here in the last few sentences as well as at the beginning in reference to the fighting tomcat whose claws were surely "barely sheathed" as he kneaded her chest. This power that "broods and lights" is the God troped by the tomcat, the same power that has carved and gashed her like the arrow, the God about which we as readers do not know very much yet, but about whom Dillard's book seeks to inform us, in whatever limited way.

The scores of images and stories from the natural world that Dillard weaves together in *Pilgrim*, then, serve as a chain of tropes for God, for that "'higher power [in the universe], not influenced by our wishes, which finally decides and judges'" (203, qtd. Werner Heisenberg). In addition to the tomcat, Dillard's first chapter gives us several more important images from nature. The most important one is the vision of the frog and the giant water bug. One summer, she walked along the bank of Tinker Creek scaring frogs into the water as she went. At the end of the bank, she saw a frog halfway in the water that did not move as she approached. She says:

> I crept closer. At last I knelt on the island's winterkilled grass, lost, dumbstruck, staring at the frog in the creek just four feet away. He was a very small frog with

wide, dull eyes. And just as I looked at him, he slowly crumpled and began to sag. The spirit vanished from his eyes as if snuffed. His skin emptied and drooped; his very skull seemed to collapse and settle like a kicked tent. He was shrinking before my eyes like a deflating football. I watched the taut, glistening skin on his shoulders tuck, and rumple, and fall. Soon, part of his skin, formless as a pricked balloon, lay in floating folds like bright scum on top of the water; it was a monstrous and terrifying thing. An oval shadow hung in the water behind the drained frog; then the shadow glided away. The frog skin bag started to sink. (5–6)

The oval shadow behind the frog was a giant water bug, an insect that seizes its victims with its front legs, bites them and injects a poison that liquifies everything inside the body except the skin. Through the puncture, "the giant water bug sucks out the victim's body, reduced to a juice" (6). Dillard says that she often returns to the spot where she saw the frog being sucked up by the giant water bug. "I'm drawn to this spot," she says, "I come to it as an oracle; I return to it as a man years later will seek out the battlefield where he lost a leg or an arm" (5). The significance of this story is that, in this "monstrous and terrifying" vision of the giant water bug, we are given another trope for God, or another indication of the kind of God that created the world. This horrific vision is maintained alongside other, more beatific visions of sharks roiling in the waves of the ocean, reflecting the light, and a mockingbird in a graceful freefall from the top of a building. Both the beautiful and the monstrous are proffered as clues to the kind of power that drives the universe and its multitude of forms, seasons, cycles, and vast stretches of nothingness.

Random acts of beauty and horror in the natural world, then, serve as data from which Dillard derives categories of meaning and indications of the nature of God. Her goal in *Pilgrim* is to "take a wider view" of the landscape of the world, to passively receive its images in their fullness, and try to determine what kind of power fashioned it. She sees herself as an explorer and a stalker, whose primary methodology is, simply, seeing. Thus, the second chapter is entitled "Seeing," and in it she talks of two primary modes of seeing and the potential they have for knowledge and mystical experience. In the first mode, one is like a blind man at a ballgame who needs a radio. The vision is accompanied by a running commentary and a degree of self-consciousness. "When I see this way," she says, "I analyze and pry. I hurl over logs and roll away stones; I study the bank a square foot at a time, probing and tilting my head" (31). This way of seeing has its benefits, but cannot match the experience that comes when one sees in a way that lets go of the commentary, self-consciousness, and analysis. "When I see this way," she says, "I sway transfixed and emptied" (31). She goes on:

> The difference between the two ways of seeing is the difference between walking with a camera and without a camera. When I walk with a camera I walk from shot to shot, reading the light on a calibrated meter. When I walk without a camera, my own shutter opens, and the moment's light prints on my own silver gut. When I see this second way I am above all an unscrupulous observer. (31)

The second way of seeing is a more passive way in that it does not involve "arranging the shot." Whatever is being seen is seen as it is, as it happens, with no interference from the observer, and the result is an epiphany of sorts. She says:

> I walk out: I see something, some event that would otherwise have been utterly missed and lost; or something sees me, some enormous power brushes me with its clean wing, and I resound like a beaten bell. (12)

Dillard's comments here about seeing, and later comments she makes about the difference between self-consciousness and consciousness, are similar to Simone Weil's remarks on the nature and spiritual value of concentration. In her essay, "Reflections on the Right Use of School Studies with a View to the Love of God", Weil argues that the faculty of attention is *the* central aspect of both school study and prayer. School study, when done with this realization in mind, has the potential to be "as good a road to sanctity as any other" (Weil 1951, 109). Any act of genuine attention or concentration, such as working a mathematics problem, has benefit on the spiritual plane regardless of whether one solves the problem. To genuinely pay attention to something is a great effort, and is often confused with certain physical effects like furrowed brows and pursed lips; genuine attention, however, is hindered by these effects. "Attention consists," Weil says,

> of suspending our thought, leaving it detached, empty, ready to be penetrated by the object . . . above all our thought should be empty, waiting, not seeking anything, but ready to receive in its naked truth the object that is to penetrate it . . . we do not obtain the most precious gifts by going in search of them but by waiting for them . . . Every school exercise, thought of in this way, is like a sacrament. (112)

For both Dillard and Weil, the observer or student is to suspend her own inner chatter and give full attention to what is before her, or, in Dillard's case, to what might come into view. The object's own "naked truth" is to be given priority over whatever conceptions or knowledge the viewer or student has of it. Weil makes this point most poignantly when she argues that the faculty of attention enables one to truly love one's neighbor. She mentions the first legend of the Grail, in which the Grail is given to the first one who asks the terribly wounded guard, "'What are you going through?'" (115). In order to love the neighbor, one must be able to ask this question and have the capacity, in terms of attention and focus, to listen to the answer. One must be able to look at the neighbor in a certain way:

> This way of looking is first of all attentive. The soul empties itself of all its own contents in order to receive into itself the being it is looking at, just as he is, in all his truth. Only he who is capable of attention can do this. (115)

These are Weil's words, but they might just as well be Dillard's, for it is this posture of emptiness and attention that she maintains throughout *Pilgrim* as she looks, not at human neighbors, but at the "neighbors" in the natural world: rocks, trees, birds, muskrats, insects, parasites, bacteria, anything. It is while looking in this way—open, waiting, emptied—that she sees the tree with the lights in it, the second primary vision around which the book is oriented (the first being the giant water bug drinking the frog). She had been walking along thinking of nothing in particular when she saw the cedar in her backyard:

> [It was] charged and transfigured, each cell buzzing with flame. I stood on the grass with the lights in it, grass that was wholly fire, utterly focused and utterly dreamed. It was less like seeing than like being for the first time seen, knocked breathless by a powerful glance. (Dillard 1974, 33)

This vision of beauty along with the vision of horror given by the giant water bug serve as primary images, around which other images and stories narrated in the book cluster and are categorized. Later, we will see that there is some degree of overlap between the two poles of beauty and horror. As she puts it, "[t]error and beauty insoluble are a ribband of blue woven into the fringes of garments of things both great and small" (24).

Dillard's Neoplatonism and the mystical cast she gives to it are not lost in these early chapters. She begins the book with an epigraph from Heraclitus: "It ever was, and is, and shall be, ever-living Fire, in measures being kindled and in measures going out." Here we have a foundation for a view of the world as bits of flame coming and going incessantly from the Fire, the One from which the many proceed. Throughout the first chapters—and the entire book—she pays special attention to light on the landscape, or light as it is reflected on whatever she views, or how reflected light makes objects visible in the first place. She often describes the play of light on an object as a flame or fire, as she does when she describes the tree with the lights in it. She speaks of the sun as the one light and source of power in our world, and decides that light has a force, as do solar winds in deep space. She says:

> I cannot cause light; the most I can do is try to put myself in the path of its beam. It is possible, in deep space, to sail on solar wind. Light, be it particle or wave, has force; you rig a giant sail and go. The secret of seeing is to sail on solar wind. Hone and spread your spirit till you yourself are a sail, whetted, translucent, broadside to the merest puff. (33)

Here, she blends, on the one hand, her understanding of the world as containing visions and bits of flame and light from the one primary source, with, on the other hand, her intention to see the world as clearly as possible by passively receiving it as it is, and letting the lighted sights take her where they will as if she herself were a sail.

So far in the book, God is the power that "broods and lights" and gashes with lightning, the source of light that illumines the random acts of beauty that are performed daily in nature whether or not one sees them. God is the one who pummels us with claws "barely sheathed," a force that knocks us breathless "with a powerful glance." God is the light that not only illumines, but does so with such fevered radiance that "we all walk about carefully averting our faces, this way and that, lest our eyes be blasted forever" (23). Dillard takes these early gleanings and moves her attention to the world of insects, which provides the natural ground from which to round out the picture of God a bit more fully.

Her meditation on insects in chapter 4, "The Fixed," begins with an account of praying mantises, who eat "more or less everything that breathes and is small enough to capture," including bees, butterflies, small snakes and rodents, even hummingbirds (55). She remembers watching, while in elementary school, mantises hatch from an egg case into a Mason jar, and eventually eat each other. The importance of mantises as a trope for God is hinted at when she describes the young mantises coming out of the egg case.

> I watched the newly hatched mantises emerge and shed their skins; they were spidery and translucent, all over joints. They trailed from the egg case to the base of the Mason jar in a living bridge that looked like Arabic calligraphy, some baffling text from the Koran inscribed down the air by a fine hand. (55)

Mantises here are compared to a sacred text, in keeping with Dillard's idea that nature is a book written upon by God, a sacred text of mysteries. Moreover, the sacred text to which Dillard compares the mantises—the *Qu'ran*—is one which holds to, above all else, a sovereign God of power.[2]

She goes on to describe the mating practices of mantises, citing the expertise of entomologist J. Henri Fabre. She explains:

> [A] chemical produced in the head of the male insect says, in effect, "No, don't go near her, you fool, she'll eat you alive." At the same time a chemical in his abdomen says, "Yes, by all means, now and forever yes." While the male is making up what passes for his mind, the female tips the balance in her favor by eating his head. He mounts her. (57–8)

While the male fertilizes the female, she continues to eat what remains of him. Such astonishing rites, commonplace in the natural world—"a world covered in chitin, where implacable realities hold sway" (59)—lead Dillard to declare in the middle of the chapter:

> Fish gotta swim and bird gotta fly; insects, it seems, gotta do one horrible thing after another. . . . More than one insect—the possibility of fertile reproduction—is an assault on all human value, all hope of a reasonable god (63).

To further amplify such an "assault on all human value," she quotes Fabre who tells the story of the Philanthus, a bee-eating wasp, who has killed a honeybee:

> If the bee is heavy with honey, the wasp squeezes its crop "so as to make her disgorge the delicious syrup, which she drinks by licking the tongue which her unfortunate victim, in her death agony, sticks out of her mouth at full length. . . . At the moment of some such horrible banquet, I have seen the Wasp, with her prey, seized by the Mantis: the bandit was rifled by another bandit. And here is an awful detail: while the Mantis held her transfixed under the points of the double saw and was already munching her belly, the Wasp continued to lick the honey of her Bee, unable to relinquish the delicious food even amid the terrors of death. Let us hasten to cast a veil over these horrors." (63–4, qtd. Fabre)

Dillard quickly makes the point that, in nature, there is no veil cast over these horrors. Rather, these mysteries are carried out for all to see and, moreover, "[t]he earth devotes an overwhelming proportion of its energy to these buzzings and leaps in the grass, to these brittle gnawings and crawlings about" (64). Given this privilege—given the givenness of insects—she only half-jokingly suggests that she keep a giant water bug on her dresser in an aquarium, so she will not forget this horrific reality. Or, maybe we should display praying mantises in churches, as a sign, to keep ourselves from casting a veil over these horrors, to insure that we do not forget what kind of world it is in which we live. Furthermore, we are not to forget what kind of God fashioned such a world. In short, the insect world, in which so many of them seem disposable, is "the brainchild of a deranged manic-depressive with limitless capital" (65). She goes on:

> If, as Heraclitus suggests, god, like an oracle, neither "declares nor hides, but sets forth by signs," then clearly I had better be scrying the signs. . . . This is what the sign of the insects says. No form is too gruesome, no behavior too grotesque, (64–5)

The fixed, mindless nature of these gruesome realities leads Dillard to claim, at first, that "the fixed is the world without fire—dead flint, dead tinder, and nowhere a spark" (67–8). This is a significant statement, given that it is made by a Neoplatonist who works within the presupposition that all the world is an emanation in flame from the One source of light. Apparently, at least initially, the bizarre and shockingly amoral actions and rites of the insects seem entirely too alien to have come from the same source as the mockingbird in free fall, or the tree with the lights in it, or the roiling sharks in the translucent wave. By the middle of the chapter, however, Dillard is rethinking her initial response to the fixed mindlessness of insects. She asks, "Where do I get my standards that I fancy the fixed world of insects doesn't meet?" (69). She concludes, contrary to Van Gogh, that the world is not "'a study that didn't come off,'" and that the fixed world of insects is where "the twin oceans of beauty and horror meet" (69). As usual, she illustrates this realization with a symbol from nature. The moon, she says, "hangs fixed and full in the east, enormously scrubbed and simple" (70). The moon, like the insects, is fixed and mindless. Granted, the moon is not the ghastly sight that many insects are; however, it is juxtaposed often enough to the sun—the inexhaustible source of light and symbol of the divine—so that it can join the insects in the category of things that, supposedly, do not qualify as sources of light, fire, or revelation. Yet, Kepler knows better from his experiments with the moon. Dillard quotes him:

> "I was engaged in other experiments with mirrors, without thinking of the warmth;
> I involuntarily turned to see whether someone was breathing on my hand." It was
> warmth from the moon. (71)

Fixed features of the natural world, then, *do* exhibit warmth and light, they *do* contain a spark of the divine, and they cannot be ignored or veiled when using the natural world as a symbol for deity. The beauty of the tree with the lights in it and the gore of the mantises come from the same source; they are emanations with a common origin.[3]

That beauty and horror come from the same source, or reflect the same deity, is a theme Dillard emphasizes later in chapter 8, entitled "Intricacy." She begins the chapter staring at her goldfish, Ellery, for whom she paid twenty-five cents. She remembers that she once looked at a goldfish's tail under a microscope and saw its red blood cells coursing through the capillaries like a red creek. She knows that Ellery's cells are streaming through his tail as she looks at him, and imagines that "if [she] concentrate[s] enough [she] might be able to feel in [her] fingers' capillaries the small knockings and flow of those circular dots, like a string of beads drawn through [her] hand" (125). She continues looking at the fishbowl and at the plant—an elodea—that floats in it. She once looked at it under a microscope, too, and saw chloroplasts bearing chlorophyll circling around each cell:

> they shone, they swarmed in ever-shifting files around and around the edge of the
> cell; they wandered, they charged, they milled, raced, and ran at the edge of
> apparent nothingness, the empty-looking inner cell; they flowed and trooped
> greenly, up against the vegetative wall. (126)

She adds that each molecule of chlorophyll is made up of over a hundred various atoms arranged in specific ways. Staring at the twenty-five-cent goldfish in his bowl, she thinks:

> A whirling air in his swim bladder balances the goldfish's weight in the water; his
> scales overlap, his feathery gills pump and filter; his eyes work, his heart beats,
> his liver absorbs, his muscles contract in a wave of extending ripples. The daphnias
> he eats have eyes and jointed legs. The algae the daphnias eat have green cells
> stacked like checkers or winding in narrow ribbons like spiral staircases up long
> columns of emptiness. And so on diminishingly down. We have not found the dot

so small it is uncreated, as it were, like a metal blank, or merely roughed in—and we never shall. (127)

The point of this close look at the goldfish in his bowl is that "[t]he creator ... churns out the intricate texture of least works that is the world with a spendthrift genius and an extravagance of care" (127). The point is that we are set down in a world in which all things are utterly gratuitous, including ourselves. "The giant water bug's predations, the frog's croak, the tree with the lights in it are not in any real sense necessary per se to the world or to its creator. Nor am I" (129). A most important fact about such a world is the detail itself, the detail with which it has been fashioned. Dillard here evokes a kabbalistic phrase—the Mystery of the Splintering of the Vessels—which refers "to the shrinking or imprisonment of essences within the various husk-covered forms of emanation or time" (129). She says,

> The Vessels splintered and solar systems spun; ciliated rotifers whirled in still water, and newts with gills laid tracks in the silt-bottomed creek. Not only did the Vessels splinter; they splintered exceedingly fine. Intricacy, then, is the subject, the intricacy of the created world. (129)

Her Neoplatonism is showing again; however, this time it comes in the form of kabbalism.[4] Her point at these early moments in the chapter "Intricacy" is not that there are emanations from the creator in nature—that is a given—but that the emanations are ubiquitous, meticulously detailed, and utterly unnecessary. Furthermore, alongside the fact of intricacy, there is another claim that can be made about the creator and the creation:

> Look, in short, at practically anything—the coot's feet, the mantis's face, a banana, the human ear—and see that not only did the creator create everything, but that he is apt to create *anything*. He'll stop at nothing. (135)

Such extravagance holds not only for form and design, but behavior as well. The mantis who eats her mate, the wasp sucking the honeybee, the water bug drinking the frog, the spider imprisoning the hummingbird—all these are given free rein in the natural world, a world in which anything goes. Not only is there no veil cast over these horrors, they, in fact, seem to be the rule: the more ghastly, lunatic and bizarre, the better. She says of the creator:

> The creator goes off on one wild, specific tangent after another, or millions simultaneously, with an exuberance that would seem to be unwarranted, and with an abandoned energy sprung from an unfathomable font. What is going on here? The point of the dragonfly's terrible lip, the giant water bug, birdsong, or the beautiful dazzle and flask of sunlighted minnows, is not that it all fits together like clockwork—for it doesn't, particularly, not even inside the goldfish bowl—

but that it all flows so freely wild, like the creek, that it all surges in such a free, fringed tangle. Freedom is the world's water and weather, the world's nourishment freely given, its soil and sap: and the creator loves pizzazz. (137)

As a curb to what many readers may think is Dillard's obsessiveness concerning the myriad of details about the created world, she asserts that her goal is not simply to learn the names of everything that has been created, but to remain open to their possible meaning, "to try to impress [her]self at all times with the fullest possible force of their reality"; she says, "I want to have things as multiply and intricately as possible present and visible in my mind" (137). Here again is the openness to the stranger—and the emptying of the self to facilitate that openness—that earlier was shown to be reminiscent of Simone Weil's ideas about concentration. Dillard's goal here is to learn the landscape of the natural world, to glean from it categories of truth, and to learn her own meaning, having been set down in the biting, flying, chomping, and snapping middle of it all. Furthermore, keeping the texture of such a world in mind, she says, "trains me to the wild and extravagant nature of the spirit I seek" (139). This spirit is God.

Dillard concludes that "nature [and by extension, God] seems to exult in abounding radicality, extremism, anarchy," that "the whole creation is one lunatic fringe," and that "[n]o claims of any and all revelations could be as far-fetched as a single giraffe" (144). The natural world is a world in which endless possibilities and complexities hold, a world replete in forms of behavior, a world steeped in intricacy. "The wonder is," she says:

given the errant nature of freedom and the burgeoning of texture in time—the wonder is that all the forms are not monsters, that there is beauty at all, grace gratuitous, pennies found, like the mockingbird's free fall. Beauty itself is the fruit of the creator's exuberance that grew such a tangle, and the grotesques and horrors bloom from that same free growth, that intricate scramble and twine up and down the conditions of time. This, then, is the extravagant landscape of the world, given, given with pizzazz, given in good measure, pressed down, shaken together, and running over. (146)

God as the creator, in these chapters, is the source of both beauty and horror; God is represented by the splendor in the natural world as well as by the alarmingly amoral, extreme, and anarchistic modes of behavior of insects.[5] The strange and alien lives of the insects give us a hint of the alien nature of the one who fashioned them.

Insects continue to fascinate Dillard as *Pilgrim* continues. She begins chapter 10, entitled "Fecundity," with the scene of two luna moths mating.[6] The male "was on top of the female, hunching repeatedly with a horrible animal vigor," and together they formed "the perfect picture of utter spirituality and utter degradation" (159–60). She intends the chapter to be a meditation on fecundity in the natural world, and the fact that it so appalls us, at least among animals (as opposed to plants). She supposes that the appalling thing about fecundity is

> the teeming evidence that birth and growth, which we value, are ubiquitous and blind, that life itself is so astonishingly cheap, that nature is as careless as it is bountiful, and that with extravagance goes a crushing waste that will one day include our own cheap lives, Henle's loops and all. (160)

One can take an optimistic, holistic stance and call this process of birth, growth and death simply, 'regeneration'; Dillard, however, plans to play "the devil's advocate and call it rank fecundity—and say that it's hell that's a-poppin'" (161).[7] She admits that her picture of the world that emphasizes beauty, complexity, and infinite detail is a pleasing picture, but is one that lies by omission. What is left out is that

> [i]t is not one pine I see, but a thousand. I myself am not one, but legion. And we are all going to die. In this repetition of individuals is a mindless stutter, an imbecilic fixedness that must be taken into account. The driving force behind all this fecundity is a terrible pressure I also must consider, the pressure of birth and growth . . . that hungers and lusts and drives the creature relentlessly toward its own death. (161)

She asks her reader to consider the rock barnacle, for example. An average barnacle lives about four years and continually reproduces itself by hatching millions of tiny larva into the water, so much that "the barnacles encrusting a single mile of shore can leak into the water a million million larvae" (166). Thinking of these milky clouds of larvae, she then asks,

> Can I fancy that a million million human infants are more real? What if God has the same affectionate disregard for us that we have for barnacles? I don't know if each barnacle larvae is of itself unique and special, or if we the people are essentially as interchangeable as bricks. . . . I have hatched, too, with millions of my kind, into a milky way that spreads from an unknown shore. (166–7)

She goes on to talk of the reproductive rates of wasps, aphids and goldfish. One single aphid (which, apparently, can reproduce without a partner), left alone for one year would produce enough offspring to stretch twenty-five hundred light years. The average goldfish lays five thousand eggs, "which she will eat as fast as she lays, if permitted" (167). Dillard tells more stories learned from Edward Way Teale's book *The Strange Lives of Familiar Insects*[8]—stories of dragonfly nymphs which eat other nymphs; mother lacewings who pause in their egg-laying to eat their eggs, lay more eggs, then eat them as well; flatworms who, in a cannibalistic frenzy, eat their own severed body parts which were in the process of regenerating. Insects do not have a monopoly on this behavior; she tells of mother predator cats who begin eating their newborn cubs as they lick the bloody umbilical cord. Just as horrifying as parents eating their offspring is the reverse: offspring eating their parents, which happens as often. In the case of gall gnats and the *Miastor* fly, sometimes the larvae hatch from eggs *within* the bodies of the adults, terribly hungry larvae who split the bellies of their parents and begin to eat the first thing in sight, usually their parent. Thinking of these things, Dillard says, she feels like Ezra: "'And when I heard this thing, I rent my garment and my mantle, and plucked off the hair of my head and of my beard, and sat down astonied'" (171).

Dillard wonders if the power in the universe—the creator—is dealing in life, or in death. She compares the creator to the manager of Southern Railroad, who needs three engines to run a particular stretch of track. The manager, then, orders that nine thousand engines be built, nine thousand very intricate, very complex engines. All nine thousand are then sent out on runs, although no one is at the throttle or is controlling the switches; the engines are utterly free and are running on the same track. They crash and burn in a terrible wreck. Only three remain, and the initial demand for three engines is supplied. The manager of the railroad—and the creator of the universe—see all but three of the nine thousand engines, and all but a few of the trillions of insect eggs [and humans, perhaps] as expendable. Dillard concludes, "Evolution loves death more than it loves you or me. . . . We value the individual supremely, and nature values him not a whit" (176). Evolution, here, serves as an example of the activity of God in nature, and it is a process that is blind, impartial, and relentless.[9]

In assertions such as these, readers begin to see the difference between the God, Dillard is envisioning and the various models of God offered by contemporary political theologies, especially feminist theologies like McFague's. Up to this point in the book, Dillard simply has looked at the landscape and seen both beauty and horror; she has concluded that both grow from the same source. This is a manageable perspective—safe, docile—as long as one is merely looking at it. The horrors in nature can even become beautiful in a certain light. However, Dillard has to forego this optimistic view when it becomes clear after looking long enough that we, as humans, cannot merely look, but are implicated in this world in which beauty and horror spring from the same root. We are implicated in that we do not enjoy privileged status among the rest of creation. We are not segregated from the rest of the creation by the creator. We humans are designed to die by the millions, for no apparent reason, and often at the hands of some other microscopic entity in the creation that is not more disposable than are we ourselves. In short, the universe is not anthropocentric. Granted, McFague argues against anthropocentrism in theology and worldview; however, for all her argumentation against it, her theology ends up being anthropocentric in that it vigorously maintains a deity that has human political, social and economic concerns at heart. In McFague's theology, and in the large body of feminist theology fashioned after it, humans do not die by the millions, like so many aphids, with God's blessing; however, this is a given in Dillard's view, a view which shares McFague's insistence on locating the divine in nature.

Dillard cannot retain the naivete of her initial look at the world, a naivete present in McFague's thought. Dillard has to look closer and acknowledge

> that the sea is a cup of death and the land is a stained altar stone. We the living are survivors huddled on flotsam, living on jetsam. We are escapees. We wake in terror, eat in hunger, sleep with a mouthful of blood. (175)

The reality and inevitability of death enters into Dillard's picture of the world, and the whole spectacle takes on a different hue. Her meditation on fecundity has added this element of death to the former picture of intricacy and multiplicity of forms and, now, "the shadows are deeper. Extravagance takes on a sinister, wastrel air, and exuberance blithers . . . it is death that is spinning the globe" (179–80). The two branches of beauty and horror, of life and death, have as their source, simply, freedom. She concludes:

> We could have planned things more mercifully, perhaps, but our plan would never get off the drawing board until we agreed to the very compromising terms that are the only ones that being offers. The world has signed a pact with the devil; it had to. It is a covenant to which every thing, even every hydrogen atom is bound. The terms are clear: if you want to live, you have to die; you cannot have mountains and creeks without space, and space is a beauty married to a blind man. The blind man is Freedom, or Time, and he does not go anywhere without his great dog Death. The world came into being with the signing of the contract. . . . This is what we know. The rest is gravy. (180–1)

That humans do not live segregated from the natural world, in which the idea of the individual is prized more than the individual herself, is a theme Dillard reasserts in chapter 13, entitled "The Horns of the Altar." She begins the chapter by telling about the time she watched a mosquito land on and suck blood from a copperhead lying placidly on a rock. Seeing this highly poisonous and dangerous snake being depleted by a tiny insect prompts her to decide that life in the world means having to be eaten. She says:

> Here was a new light on the intricate texture of things in the world, the actual plot of the present moment in time after the fall: the way we the living are nibbled and nibbling—not held aloft on a cloud in the air but bumbling pitted and scarred and broken through a frayed and beautiful land. (227)

The label "the living" brings to mind the title of Dillard's novel *The Living*, and the striking themes of struggle and death that pervade the book, themes that will be discussed later. Here, Dillard is preoccupied with the idea of wholeness being devitalized by being eaten or nibbled, in this case, by parasites. She begins her meditation on parasitism by saying, quite frankly, that "being parasitized is a way of life—if you call that a living" (228). She remembers being given a book about insects, including parasites, that read like "the devil's *summa theologica*" (229). Her connection between the lives of parasites and a theological text reiterates her conviction that the natural world is, in itself, a profound religious text. Additional reading teaches Dillard that of all the world's species, ten percent are parasitic. Thinking of God as an inventor, she asks:

> What if you were an inventor, and you made ten percent of your inventions in such a way that they could only work by harassing, disfiguring, or totally destroying the other ninety percent? These things are not well enough known. (229)

She then begins a litany of several pages, detailing aspects of the lives of various parasitic species, such as lice, fleas, flies, wasps, beetles, moths, ticks, and worms. Parasites are so abundant that, for example, "there is . . . a species of louse for almost every species of everything else," and "there are over one hundred thousand species of parasitic wasps . . . [so many] that some parasitic wasps have parasitic wasps" (229–32). Parasites spend their lives in the bodies of their hosts: in their horns, nostrils, intestines, ears, hair follicles, and eyes; between their fingers, on the edge of their lips, in their brains, or on their wings. Dillard decides:

> Certainly we give our infants the wrong idea about their fellow creatures in the world. Teddy bears should come with tiny stuffed bear-lice; ten percent of all baby bibs and rattles sold should be adorned with colorful blowflies, maggots and screw-worms. . . . Could it be, counting bacteria and viruses, that we live in a world in which half the creatures are running from—or limping from—the other half? (233)

What this tells her about God is that "the creator is no puritan. A creature need not work for a living; creatures may simply steal and suck and be blessed for all that with a share—an enormous share—of the sunlight and air" (233). Parasitism is a testament to the "manic exuberance" of the creator; furthermore, it is the rent paid by all creatures who live in the world, a reiteration, in itself, of the fact that "the world is actual and fringed, pierced here and there, and through and through, with the toothed conditions of time and the mysterious, coiled spring of death" (234). The living, including humans,

> are eating each other . . . we're all in this Mason jar together, snapping at anything that moves. . . . out here on the rocks the people don't mean to grapple, to crush and starve and betray, but with all the good will in the world, we do, there's no other way. We want it; we take it out of each other's hides; we chew the bitter skins the rest of our lives. (239–40)

The phrase "out here on the rocks" calls to mind Dillard's essay entitled "Life on the Rocks," which will be discussed later. The essay reminds the reader of the point Dillard makes here: as humans, we are again not exempt from the parasitic life, in that we ourselves both eat and are eaten, harm and are harmed. We are implicated and involved in this aspect of the natural world; we are not protected from those parasites, viruses, and bacteria that would thrive in us and kill us, nor are we held aloft so that we rise above parasitic rites ourselves. The God who has created the world under such conditions, apparently, is no bleeding heart; the creator does not flinch or blink at these dread realities, nor does s/he intervene to change them or to save us from them.

Again, Dillard corrects her vision, taking in more of the landscape as it is rather than she might wish it to be. She realizes that the cedar tree with the lights in it was probably covered in malignant galls, although its transfigured beauty remains in her memory. The free-falling mockingbird probably had lice of several sorts, and the roiling, lighted sharks were probably gashed and scarred from violent encounters with rocks, predators, or each other. She turns to herself, speaking of an illness she had: "If the pneumococcus bacteria had flourished more vitally, if it had colonized my other lung successfully, living and being fruitful after its kind, then I would have died my death" (239). To live and be fruitful—these are the words of blessing given by the creator to all living things; yet for some things to live and be fruitful requires that other equally worthy and beautiful things must die often excruciating and violent deaths. In this creator's economy, a child is no less expendable, nor more precious, than a virus. Dillard declares:

> I am a frayed and nibbled survivor in a fallen world, and I am getting along. I am aging and eaten and have done my share of eating too. I am not washed and beautiful, in control of a shining world in which everything fits, but instead am wandering awed about on a splintered wreck I've come to care for, whose gnawed trees breathe a delicate air, whose bloodied and scarred creatures are my dearest companions, and whose beauty beats and shines not *in* its imperfections but overwhelmingly in spite of them, under the wind-rent clouds, upstream and down. (242)

She concludes the chapter by envisioning herself as a sacrifice strapped "to the horns of the world's rock altar" (242). She has already, in a previous chapter, called the land a stained altar stone, stained in the blood of all who wish to live in it. Here, lying on the altar, she sees that the horns themselves have worms in them. She waits for the worms to come and eat her, but suddenly the cords loose and she walks away. She escapes, at least this time. By envisioning herself as a sacrifice on the world's—or God's—altar, she demonstrates a particular spiritual posture which defines her approach to God and religious meaning. She is willing to be eaten, blasted, or sacrificed if that is what is required to truly live in and be mindful of the actual world. Preconceived notions of the world or God are sacrificed willingly for a chance to even touch the hem of the garment of what is true about the actual world and our lives in it. Her sacrificial posture also hearkens back to the mode of passivity discussed earlier in this chapter. The passivity of a sacrificial victim is an indicator of the victim's submission to the sacrifice as being integral to "the way things are" in the world. Dillard, as an imaginary sacrificial victim, submits to the realities of parasites, viruses, and bacteria, and their rival claims to life. She submits to the fact that the world operates not according to human conceptions of goodness, fairness, or economy, but according to the deranged plan of a lunatic creator. The world we call "ours" is a theocentric one and, in the end, "'there is a higher power, not influenced by our wishes, that finally decides and judges'" (203, quoting Werner Heisenberg).

Dillard's posture of passivity, as hinted earlier in the chapter, is connected to her views of consciousness and self-consciousness. To be self-conscious is to be too tuned in to one's own self to truly see, hear or pay attention to who or what is immediately visible. To be simply conscious is to lose that blind egoistic vision and to really see and be filled with the spectacle. Dillard experiences this kind of loss of self-consciousness throughout *Pilgrim*; however, in chapter 11, entitled "Stalking," her self-consciousness is lost while she is stalking various animals, especially muskrats. In this chapter, she tells of trying to see animals determined to hide themselves, by trying to put herself in their paths. She spends a considerable section of the chapter talking about techniques for stalking muskrats, things that have worked for her, things that failed. She tells of the incredible rush of feeling she experiences when these forays into the woods pay off, and she is allowed rare glimpses of muskrats feeding and swimming. Her description of what goes on inside her when she sees a muskrat further underscores the importance of a posture of passivity and non-self-consciousness, even when engaged in an activity such as stalking:

> In my brain I am not saying, Muskrat! Muskrat! There! I am saying nothing. If I
> must hold a position, I do not "freeze." If I freeze, locking my muscles, I will tire
> and break. Instead of going rigid, I go calm. I center down wherever I am; I find
> a balance and repose. I retreat—not inside myself, but outside myself, so that I
> am a tissue of sense. Whatever I see is plenty, abundance. I am the skin of water
> the wind plays over; I am petal, feather, stone. (201)

Dillard gives her attention to the muskrats not by tensing her muscles, like the students Simone Weil speaks of who furrow their brows when they try to do a geometry problem. Dillard truly sees the muskrats when she lets go of herself, loosens her body, and becomes ultra-sensitive to the muskrats, or to whatever is not herself. She becomes passive and allows herself to be played upon. This is a skill one must develop if one wants to have success in stalking. Soon, however, the attentive reader learns that Dillard is not merely talking about muskrats here; rather the muskrats serve as a trope for God or the spirit, whom she stalks as relentlessly as—and simultaneously with—the muskrats. Knowing that nature and God are, to a large degree, hidden, she compares herself to Moses, who asked God to see his glory, and was obliged only to see God's back parts. She laments the "now-you-see-it, now-you-don't" characteristic of God and of nature, but must admit that at those times when the mockingbird falls, or the tree lights up, the back parts are plenty, an abundance. As Moses' face was changed after seeing God's back parts, Dillard feels that, perhaps, her own face is changed after these encounters in nature with the spirit. The idea of a face being changed or burned will resurface later in Dillard's *Holy the Firm, Teaching a Stone to Talk,* and *The Living.*

Dillard's response, then, to the God who designed the non-anthropocentric world is not to fear this God, or to focus only on the comforting aspects of the world that indicate soothing aspects of the 'personality' of this God. Rather, she stalks this powerful God with as much skill as she can hone; she is willing to be played upon by the "thrashings of the spirit," willing to have her face burned by them. In fact, the thought of being acted upon by the power in the universe is the pinnacle of the spiritual life for Dillard. This sentiment she expresses quite graphically in chapter 12, entitled "Nightwatch," in which she describes standing in a meadow surrounded by waves of grasshoppers. She knows from her reading that ordinary grasshoppers suddenly, at a certain time in their lives, undergo a change and become locusts, and begin to migrate in voracious, devouring hordes that ruin anything in sight. She cites a passage from the Hebrew Bible that speaks of locusts as a flame that burns across the land, leaving a desolate plain. She tells another story:

> A man lay down to sleep in a horde of locusts, Will Barker says. Instantly the suffocating swarm fell on him and knit him in a clicking coat of mail. The metallic mouthparts meshed and pinched. His friends rushed in and woke him at once. But when he stood up, he was bleeding from the throat and wrists. The world has locusts, and the world has grasshoppers. I was up to my knees in the world. (209)

The man lying down in the swarm of locusts is reminiscent of Dillard laying herself down on the horns of the world's altar, which she knows is stained with blood and full of parasitic worms. The image is one of submission and sacrificial willingness— submission to an unyielding reality, and a willingness to experience that reality on whatever terms its agents offer it; in this case, at the price of a little blood here and there. Dillard continues to speak of the grasshoppers in the meadow, which spray her body as she progresses through the tall grass. She feels exhilarated:

> I was the bride who waits with her lamp filled. . . . I had come to the Lucas place to spend a night there, to let come what may . . . This is what I had come for, just this, and nothing more. A fling of leafy motion on the cliffs, the assault of real things . . . for the pleasure of being so purely played. (211–6).

She longs for the "assault," to experience the power of the real world—a world "where power and beauty hold sovereign sway"—at whatever cost (219).[10]

From her discussion of the grasshoppers, she moves to a meditation on migrating eels, about whom she heard from Edwin Way Teale. Silver eels, he says, often crawl across several miles of meadow at night on their way to the Sargasso Sea. She imagines this sight, a silver seething across a field as far as one could see. She says:

> If I saw that sight, would I live? If I stumbled across it, would I ever set foot from my door again? Or would I be seized to join that compelling rush, would I cease eating, and pale, and abandon all to start walking? . . . This, the whole story of the eels at which I have only just hinted, is extravagant in the extreme, and food for another kind of thought, a thought about the meaning of such wild, incomprehensible gestures. (220)

Clearly, such thought is the kind Dillard engages in throughout the entirety of *Pilgrim*, for her quest is to ascertain meaning from such sights and events in nature. Furthermore, readers are given to conclude that Dillard, if she saw the migrating eels, would opt to go with them, just as she might consider laying down in a field of swarming locusts. It is the assault she craves, after all:

> I cannot ask for more than to be so wholly acted upon, flown at, and lighted on in throngs, probed, knocked, even bitten. A little blood from the wrists and throat is the price I would willingly pay for that pressure of clacking weights on my shoulders, for the scent of deserts, groundfire in my ears— for being so in the clustering thick of things, rapt and enwrapped in the rising and falling real world. (221)

The "rising and falling" here is a hint of the neoplatonic vision of the world as an emanation from and to the One; furthermore, it recalls the epigraph of the book from Heraclitus, about the world as a flame forever going in and coming out. These grasshoppers and eels, for Dillard, are flames of emanation coming in and going out, falling and rising emanations of material spirit that she stalks and in which she immerses herself in order to experience the power of the universe. Blood at the throat and wrists is Dillard's version of stigmata, marks of her brand of spirituality.

Dillard speaks again, in chapter 14, "Northing," of the death of the self that is required if one is to have spiritual experiences in nature like those she has spent the entirety of *Pilgrim* recounting. She says:

> The death of the self of which the great writers speak is no violent act. It is merely the joining of the great rock heart of the earth in its roll. It is merely the slow cessation of the will's sprints and the intellect's chatter; it is waiting like a hollow bell with a stilled tongue. (258)[11]

Waiting is of key importance, in both stalking muskrats and in tracking the spirit. She says:

> Not only does something come if you wait, but it pours over you like a waterfall, like a tidal wave. You wait in all naturalness, without expectation or hope, emptied, translucent, and that which comes rocks and topples you; it will shear, loose, launch, winnow, grind. (259)

Encountering muskrats—or God—is an experience of being ground and rocked. One puts oneself in the path of God—on the altar, for example—and waits for the knife of sacrifice to begin its task. At the end of the chapter, standing under the November sky and feeling the cold wind, Dillard thinks of the Israelite wave offering, in which the priest waves the breast of an unblemished ram before God in thanksgiving. She concludes, "the wind's knife has done its work. Thanks be to God" (259). Again, she offers herself as the sacrificial victim to the spirit in order to experience the full force of the power that "broods and lights."

In the last chapter, entitled "The Waters of Separation," Dillard mentions another kind of Israelite offering, the heave offering.[12] The heaved shoulder offering is done at the same time as the wave breast offering of thanksgiving. She wonders if the priest heaves the shoulder of the consecrated ram *at* the Lord, as if to say "God *look* what you've done to this creature, look at the sorrow, the cruelty, the long damned waste! . . . How high, how far, could I heave a little shred of frog shoulder at the Lord?" (264). The frog shoulder is, of course, the shoulder of the frog that was sucked dry by the giant water bug, the frog that had its beginnings in a pod of thousands of eggs, only a few of which survived. Dillard wants to heave the tiny shoulder to God as "a violent, desperate way of catching God's eye . . . [to] speak up for the creation" (264). The heave offering aids in venting the sorrow and loss that accompanies life in the world, death at the hands of the world and the natural forces that run loose within it.[13] She wonders, "How many people have prayed for their daily bread and famished? They die their daily death as utterly as did the frog, *people*, played with, dabbled upon, when God knows they loved their life" (265). God does not intervene to protect people from these violent and tragic events; in fact, it is God who toys with them. Dillard stands and remembers the "signs" she has seen in the natural world, the sign of the insects and their terrible fecundity, the parasites and their voracious appetites that render death to their hosts. These signs are grave wonders, yet they are balanced by the sign she sees in the last part of the last chapter: a twirling maple key that comes falling in front of her, being blown by the wind. The maple key is

> a creature spread thin to that other wind, the wind of the spirit which bloweth where it listeth, lighting, and raising up, and easing down . . . [it is] blown by a generous, unending breath. That breath never ceases to kindle, exuberant,

abandoned; frayed splinters spatter in every direction and burgeon into flame. (268)

The maple key is surely falling, blown, played upon like the people and the frog who die their respective deaths. Dillard decides, however, "if I am a maple key falling, at least I can twirl" (268). In short, yes, things are bound to live their short days and then fall, often in a spray of blood and violence, crashing down into the dust from whence they came. This goes for everybody—people, maples, insects, other animals. Since this is a given, then let the sparks fly, let the blood flow and let the whole show go on and out in a blast of color and flame. Rather than "to step aside from the gaps where the creeks and winds pour down," rather than remove herself from the path of those forces and powers in the universe that thrash and gash and pummel, Dillard exhorts her readers to seek these gaps. She says:

> The gaps are the thing. The gaps are the spirit's one home, the altitudes and latitudes so dazzlingly spare and clean that the spirit can discover itself for the first time like a once-blind man unbound. The gaps are the clifts in the rock where you cower to see the back parts of God . . . Go up into the gaps . . . Stalk the gaps . . . and you'll come back, for you will come back, transformed in a way you may not have bargained for—dribbling and crazed. (268–9)[14]

Again, she evokes the memory of Moses, who went up into the mountain to see God, risking his life just to stand in the presence of God, knowing that the power might just kill him. This is the daredevil spirituality Dillard preaches; moreover, it is a spirituality fashioned in response to the kind of God she sees present in nature, a God who deals in death no less than life, a God who "is not playful . . . a power that is unfathomably secret, and holy, and fleet" (270). She says of God and of life in quest for God:

> Did you think, before you were caught [caught up into a gap], that you needed, say, life? Do you think that you will keep your life, or anything else you love? But no. Your needs are all met. But not as the world giveth . . . you have learned that the outrageous guarantee holds. You see the creatures die, and you know you will die. And one day it occurs to you that you must not need life. Obviously. And then you're gone. You have finally understood that you are dealing with a maniac. (270)

What is the outrageous guarantee? That to live, you have to die, and that we will always have needs for which we receive gifts we had not bargained for. God is a maniac whose primary concern is not to provide comfort to humans. Dillard says of this reality:

> There is nothing to be done about it, but ignore it, or see. And then you walk fearlessly, eating what you must, growing wherever you can, like the monk on the

road who knows precisely how vulnerable he is, who takes no comfort among
death-forgetting men, and who carries his vision of vastness and might around in
his tunic like a live coal which neither burns him nor warms him, but with which
he will not part. (270)

For Dillard, a vision of God that prioritizes power and might, and does not ignore
the realities of death, is more honest and gives a more accurate rendering of the
world in which we live than a vision that seeks to comfort itself with visions of a
God whose delight is to succor, rescue and soothe.

Dillard ends the chapter and the book by referring again—almost word for
word from the first chapter—to the old cat she used to have, the cat who bloodied
her and sharpened his barely-sheathed claws on her chest. "I've been bloodied and
mauled, wrung, dazzled, drawn" (270), she says, speaking of her encounters with
both the cat and with God. The spiritual life—the life lived face to face with the
realities of the natural world—is a life splattered in blood and chips of bone, a life
bedazzled and blinded by beauty and flame. Dillard joins the Israelite priests who
"offered the wave breast and the heave shoulder together, freely, in full knowledge,
for thanksgiving. They waved, they heaved, and neither gesture was whole without
the other, and both meant a wide-eyed and keen-eyed thanks" (271). "Wide-eyed"
and "keen-eyed" are necessary traits for anyone who wishes to truly see the world,
for it is too easy to simply shield oneself from its gruesome realities, and the
implication these realities have for human life.

In *Pilgrim*, then, Dillard presents a view of the world that includes a God
conceived of in terms of extravagance, beauty, violence, and power intertwined.
This God is manifested by a myriad of entities and events in the natural world:
predatory animals, parasitic insects, microscopic organisms such as bacteria and
viruses, seasons, winds, floods, various lights from the sky, and so on. Nothing
that happens in the natural world is outside of God's purview or sanction.
Furthermore, humans are not segregated from the natural world, or exempt from
its precepts. Animals kill and eat each other—or humans—in a frenzy of torn flesh
and snapping bones; floods, winds and rains ravage the earth and destroy all life,
human or otherwise; microscopic beings tuck themselves into the folds of other
living beings, humans included, and eat more than their fill. God does not intervene
into nature on anyone's behalf, but acts via nature impartially and without regard
for human ethical, religious, political, or legal concerns. Clearly, Dillard's God is
not the same God McFague and others envision as they advance a theology for the
ecological, nuclear age—a theology that places human political, social, and
economic concerns at the forefront of the divine concern. Such concerns take on
relative importance when seen as just one more fold among the wrinkled and
intricate texture of the natural world; furthermore, the God manifested in the natural
world cannot be said to privilege the concerns of the human more than those of
any other entity in the creation. A deity of this sort is expected in the apophatic
tradition of which Dillard's work partakes. The *via negativa* as an approach to a

doctrine of God emphasizes not the nearness or revelation of God, but the otherness and dissimilarity of God to human lives and concerns. In the next chapter, we will see Dillard model deity upon the poles in the Arctic and Antarctica, poles that are extremely remote and found amidst landscapes exacting and dangerous. Dillard's focus upon distance and otherness of deity (paradoxically revealed in the near and sometimes familiar universe), and upon the horrors of the natural world lead Linda Smith to argue that the inevitable conclusion of the last half of *Pilgrim* is that "God is totally unlike humankind . . . so 'wholly other' that he does not care about the fate of human beings, whether as a race or as individuals" (28).[15] This same God resurfaces again and again in her later books, especially *Holy the Firm, Teaching a Stone to Talk*, and her novel *The Living*, to which I now turn.

Notes

1. Linda L. Smith identifies Dillard as a panentheist in correspondence with process thought (Smith 1991, 17). I agree that Dillard is a panentheist, but the characterizations of God that come from American process thinkers seem too optimistic for Dillard's taste.

2. Gary McIlroy suggests rightly that the story of the mantises in the Mason jar interrupts "order and predictability" and points to the "startling presence of nature in society" and the "intractability of the natural world, its blind disregard for the conventions of society" (McIlroy 1987, 73). Using the mantises as a trope for God, as all of nature is, I argue that God, like the mantises, interrupts order and predictability and exhibits blind disregard for societal convention.

3. See also Smith's comments on Dillard's use of light in the book to represent revelation or divine immanence (Smith 1991, 22–23).

4. For more on the relationship between kabbalah and Neoplatonism, see Gershom Scholem, *Origins of the Kabbalah* (Princeton: Jewish Publication Society, 1987): 414–54; Moshe Idel, *Kabbalah: New Perspectives* (New Haven, Conn.: Yale University Press, 1988): 136–55. See also the story entitled "The Breaking of the Vessels" in Martin Buber's *Tales of the Hasidim: The Early Masters* (New York: Schocken Books, 1947): 121.

5. Smith labels *Pilgrim* a theodicy of sorts, in that "Dillard's greatest theological challenge is to reconcile the apparently opposing aspects of God as the Creator of beauty and the Creator of horror" (18). Smith goes on to say that Dillard meets this challenge not with a simplistic rendering of God, but with "a remarkable resolution that blends traditional mysticism with modern aesthetics" (18).

6. On the issue of fecundity, the difference in perspective between Dillard and Levinas glares. In contrast to Dillard's graphic and detailed discussion of appalling fecundity, Levinas discusses the issue in terms of transcendence, erotic love, and otherness. In *Totality and Infinity* (Levinas 1969, 267–9) he explains that the birth of the child is a transcendence of transubstantiation for the parent that results in an encounter with otherness. The child, while an extension of the parent, is also other than the parent, so that in the child, the parent encounters himself as an other. I say 'himself' here because Levinas speaks almost exclusively of paternity and fatherhood. In the lectures collected in *Time and the Other*, he argues that "Paternity is the relationship with a stranger who, entirely while being Other, is myself, the relationship of the ego with a myself who is nonetheless a stranger to me" (Levinas 1987c, 91).

7. Smith suggests that Dillard's frequent use of circular imagery—the snake with its tail in its mouth, the orbits of the planets—indicates "wholeness, spiritual perfection, and the cycle of birth, death, and regeneration" (35). While acknowledging Dillard's use of circular images, it seems to me that just such a holistic view is what Dillard is trying to augment by her focus on the horror in fecundity. The sentimentality of the typical holistic vision ignores the rankness of fecundity; Dillard seeks to remind her readers of it.

8. The title of this book is interesting in that it juxtaposes the words 'strange' and 'familiar', a juxtaposition that has specific meaning when taken in a Levinasian sense. This will be discussed later.

9. Dillard uses the terms 'creator' and 'creation' at the same time that she speaks of evolutionary processes in the world, which may appear as a contradiction to some. To the extent that deity in Dillard's work is aligned with forces and powers in the natural world, the terms 'creator' and 'creation' are used loosely and for their artistic impact within her aesthetic vision of the world. They are not meant to indicate necessarily an actual deity who created everything at a specific time. Evolutionary process in the world is simply "the way things are" for Dillard. If one wants to ascribe such processes to an actual divine entity, there is room in Dillard's perspective to do so; however, her persona in her work does not insist or depend on this notion at all.

10. The word 'sovereign' here makes a small theological link between the sovereign natural/spiritual world Dillard envisions and the sovereign God of Edwardian Calvinism.

11. Dillard frequently uses bell imagery throughout *Pilgrim*. She speaks of being swung like a bell, resounding like a bell, and a bell hanging from inside her ribcage. Imagining herself as a bell reinforces the passivity and emptiness that are integral features of her brand of spirituality.

12. Goldman's article connecting *Pilgrim* to Leviticus is important to mention here. He rightly notes the "bloodiness" of the book and the landscape it describes and, further, the fact that a basic quest of the book is to determine "what kind of God resides in the bloodspattered wilderness, and how does one worship the divine" (Goldman 1991, 198). Goldman goes on to weave into this bloodbath Dillard's images of sacrifice, so that blood becomes both an agent of contamination and of cleansing.

13. Smith notes the connection between the heave offering and Dillard's love of softball and development of her throwing arm. "Dillard," she goes on to say, "transforms a ritual of worship into that common, if childish, expression of anger—throwing something" (32).

14. Mark C. Taylor uses the word 'gap' to refer to the non-site where the holy is faced. In his book *Altarity* he attempts an analysis of various texts of deconstruction to stage the traces of the holy, and approaches what some would call a religion of the gaps.

15. See my article "An Invitation from Silence: Annie Dillard's Use of the Mystical Concepts of *Via Positiva* and *Via Negativa*," *Mystics Quarterly* 19 (March 1993): 26–33. Furthermore, Smith notes that Dillard's willingness to confront the horrors of nature head-on separates her from nineteenth-century transcendentalists and places her closer to, say, Melville in *Moby Dick* than Thoreau or Emerson (43–4).

Chapter 3

God in the Landscape

The models of deity explicit in Dillard's *Pilgrim at Tinker Creek* appear again and
again in subsequent books. Dillard continues to model deity upon the landscape of
the natural world; the creek in Virginia is replaced with the barren, icy tundra of
Antarctica, the jagged coasts of the Pacific Northwest, or the windy islands of the
Galapagos. In each instance, the deity that emerges is one utterly sovereign and
wild in all directions. In this chapter, I will examine three of Dillard's books and
the models of deity that emerge from their pages.

Deity, Tragedy, and the Problem of Evil

Holy the Firm is a short book (only 67 pages of actual text). Its brevity, however,
in no way undermines its depth, for it is, from cover to cover, a substantial meditation
on time, death, suffering, nature, and God, all within the categories of esoteric
Christianity. The book was published in 1977 and records Dillard's reflections on
the events of three successive days picked at random from a host of days she spent
living in a one-room cabin in Puget Sound. Accordingly, the book is divided into
three parts, one for each day, and at the end of the first section, Dillard tells her
reader: "Nothing is going to happen in this book. There is only a little violence
here and there in the language, at the corner where eternity clips time" (24). Violence
is a permanent feature in Dillard's conception of the world, and it figures
prominently in her work and in her conceptions of the divine. In *Holy the Firm*,
violence manifests most importantly in the remembrance of a burning moth on the
first day, the burned face of a child who lives through a plane crash on the second

day, and in the potential violence directed from God against churchgoers on the third day.

Dillard begins the book by describing the day as a god. "Every day is a god," she says, "I worship each god, I praise each day splintered down, splintered down and wrapped in time like a husk, a husk of many colors spreading . . . " (11). Divinity, then, is located in and/or associated with *this* world, the world of time, space and matter. She wakes and looks out onto the Bay in Puget Sound:

> I open my eyes. The god lifts from the water. His head fills the bay. He is Puget Sound, the Pacific; his breast rises from pastures; his fingers are firs; islands slide wet down his shoulders. . . . Today's god rises, his long eyes flecked in clouds. He flings his arms, spreading colors; he arches, cupping sky in his belly; he vaults, vaulting and spread, holding all and spread on me like skin. (12)

Here is the familiar Dillardian association between divinity and the natural universe, an association that traces back to her transcendentalist, Neoplatonic forbears. She is surrounded by divinity, by the real in time and space, and today's god seems benign, spreading colors and clouds. She goes on to describe her one-room house, her cat, and the spider that lives in the corner of her bathroom, around whose web lie a dozen moth corpses. Upon seeing the corpses, Dillard remembers seeing a burning moth while she was camping in the Blue Ridge Mountains. She had been reading by candlelight and moths kept flying into the flame and falling onto her cooking pans. One moth, however, flew into the flame and got stuck in the wax. Dillard describes:

> A golden female moth, a biggish one with a two-inch wingspan, flapped into the fire, dropped her abdomen into the wet wax, stuck, flames, frazzled and fried in a second. Her moving wings ignited like tissue paper, enlarging the circle of light in the clearing . . . At once the light contracted again and the moth's wings vanished in a fine, foul smoke. At the same time, her six legs clawed, curled, blackened, and ceased, disappearing utterly. And her head jerked in spasms, making a sputtering noise; her antennae crisped and burned away and her heaving mouth parts crackled like pistol fire. When it was all over . . . [a]ll that was left was the glowing horn shell of her abdomen and thorax—a fraying, partially collapsed gold tube jammed upright in the candle's round pool. And then this moth-essence, this spectacular skeleton, began to act as a wick. She kept burning . . . She burned for two hours without changing, without bending or leaning—only glowing within . . . like a hollow saint, like a flame-faced virgin gone to God. (16–7)

The graphic description of the moth sizzling in the flames is the first instance of violence in the book. The violent and graphic passage, however, is transformed into a description of the burning moth that compares her to a saint or flame-faced virgin. Only after being scorched in the flame was the moth then able to become the wick, the channel of the flame, a holy figure. This passage and the idea contained within it—the idea that suffering and holiness are linked—will have further resonance in later passages in the book. For now, Dillard shifts into a discussion of the mountains and the sea that surround her in Puget Sound.

With the landscape of Puget Sound in mind, Dillard says: "I came here to study hard things—rock mountain and salt sea—and to temper my spirit on their edges. 'Teach me thy ways, O Lord' is, like all prayers, a rash one, and one I cannot but recommend" (19). In this statement, we see the material landscape of Puget Sound linked to the immaterial landscape of spirit, specifically Dillard's own spirit. The mountains and sea serve to temper her spirit; furthermore, studying hard things, like mountains and sea, is synonymous with prayer. In short, coming to study the mountains and sea is an effort in the interest of learning the ways of God. This is not a surprising assumption; Dillard assumes a connection between the material and immaterial throughout her work. Why, though, is "teach me thy ways, O Lord" a rash prayer? It is a rash prayer because the answer is bound up with mountains that are hard and have edges. The ways of God and the ways of the mountains are similar; for all their beauty and majesty, both embody potential danger to humans due to their jagged cliffs, high latitudes, and deadly climate. In Dillard's mind, it is no accident that the power of God is often associated with or located in or on top of a mountain. As she asserted at the end of *Pilgrim*, God is in the gaps of the mountains, hiding in the clifts of rocks, and she urges those who would know the ways of God to seek the gaps and clifts. She urges this in spite of the fact that, earlier in the book, she is not sure why "so many mystics of all creeds experience the presence of God on mountaintops" (89). She says:

> Aren't they afraid of being blown away? God said to Moses on Sinai that even the priests, who have access to the Lord, must hallow themselves, for fear that the Lord may break out against them. This is *the* fear. It often feels best to lay low, inconspicuous, instead of waving your spirit around from high places like a lightning rod. For if God is in one sense the igniter, a fireball that spins over the ground of continents, God is also in another sense the destroyer, lightning, blind power, impartial as the atmosphere. Or God is one 'G.' . . . In the open anything might happen. (89)

The God of the mountains, the God *in* the mountains is a God who, like the mountains, is impartial, which is a "hard," "rash" reality for those who prefer to think of divinity as loving and nurturing. Yet, Dillard comes to the mountains to learn about these harsh divine realities, these rough edges of the personality of God, and to "temper her spirit" on them. All prayers to God are rash because, as she maintains later, prayer takes one into the presence of God, a presence one may not survive. These grim realities, however, are not manifested immediately in the mountains on this first day of *Holy the Firm*. This comes on the second day.

On the second day, a plane snags on a fir and crashes, and the face of seven-year-old Julie Norwich is burned off. Dillard says of the day, and of the god of that

day: "It is November 19 and no wind, and no hope of heaven, and no wish for
heaven, since the meanest of people show more mercy than hounding and terrorist
gods" (36). She remembers seeing Julie two weeks before at an area gathering, the
way Julie carried her cat around and clothed him in a dress that made him look like
a nun. Thinking of Julie, now in the hospital, with no face, Dillard concludes:

> It is the best joke there is, that we are here, and fools—that we are sown into time
> like so much corn, that we are souls sprinkled at random like salt into time and
> dissolved here, spread into matter, connected by cells right down to our feet, and
> those feet likely to fell us over a tree root or jam us on a stone. The joke part is that
> we forget it. . . . The joke of the world is less like a banana peel than a rake, the old
> rake in the grass, the one you step on, foot to forehead. . . . One step on the rake
> and it's mind under matter once again. You wake up with a piece of tree in your
> skull. . . . We're tossed broadcast into time like so much grass, some ravening
> god's sweet hay. You wake up and a plane falls out of the sky. (41–4)

Human frailty and insignificance to the gods is the point here, and the fact that the
world is not made with our comfort in mind. The world is made up of material
elements against whose edges we often find ourselves pressed, scathed or killed.
Furthermore, once we die, another "crop" of humans take our places for a short
while until they, too, fall victim to the old rake trick and matter does them in as
well. They fall off a mountain, or drown, or crash into something. The god of this
second day, for Dillard, is a god who eats humans like hay, hay grown from the
soul-seeds that god threw randomly into time so they could flourish for their brief
moment, and then perish.

What about the god of the first day? Does not that benign god have power to
save? No, Dillard answers; "[t]hat day's god has no power. No gods have power to
save. There are only days. The one great god abandoned us to days, to time's
tumult of occasions, abandoned us to the gods of days each brute and amok in his
hugeness and idiocy" (43). This is a rather poignant passage for understanding the
kind of God Dillard envisions. Although God did not reach down and rip Julie
Norwich's plane out of the sky, s/he might as well have, for the one God has seen
to it that we live subject to the brute conditions of time, space and matter—none of
which have individual human comfort, happiness, or security as a telos. To those
who prefer to think of God exclusively as a God of love and peace, Dillard has
sobering words:

> [Y]ou can get caught holding one end of a love, when your father drops, and your
> mother; when a land is lost, or a time, and your friend blotted out, gone, your
> brother's body spoiled, and cold, your infant dead, and you dying; you reel out
> love's long line alone, stripped like a live wire loosing its sparks to a cloud, like a
> live wire loosed to longing and grief everlasting. (44)

God does not guarantee the longevity of anything anyone loves; God has, instead, loosed us to sojourn on a speckled earth that holds within it the possibility for death as much as life, horror as much as beauty, and pain as much as comfort. Dillard goes on:

> [W]e reel out love's long line alone toward a God less lovable than a grasshead, who treats us less well than we treat our lawns. . . . God is a brute and traitor, abandoning us to time, to necessity and the engines of matter unhinged. This is no leap; this is evidence of things seen. (46)

What she has seen, of course, is a seven-year-old whose face has been burned off for no apparent reason, which is, in itself, just one of a host of such travesties that occur on a daily basis in the world. As Dillard looks at the mountains and thinks about this second day, she determines that "[t]he god of today is a glacier. We live in his shifting crevasses, unheard. The god of today is delinquent, a barn-burner, a punk with a pittance of power in his match" (49). Looking at the mountains, she notices a peak she had not noticed before because it was hidden by haze and blue. She decides to call this peak, among other things, "God's Tooth." Of course, the new peak is a metaphor for the new, savage face of God that she has seen on this second day. The benign, vaulting god of yesterday has been replaced, or supplemented, with the ravenous, impartial, and cruel god of today's plane crash. The idea of God having teeth, furthermore, resonates with the metaphors in *Pilgrim* by which Dillard aligns God with predatory animals, so that predatory, toothed animals represent God, by proxy, due to the fact that "anything goes" in nature, in both design and behavior.

Surprisingly, Dillard begins the third section of the book—the section dealing with the third day—by stating that she "know[s] only enough of God to want to worship him, by any means ready to hand" (55). Readers might not expect such a statement given the angry tone and accusations of the last section. Nevertheless, she begins the section with a narrative about the Congregationalist church she attends, and the way in which "God burgeons up or showers down into the shabbiest of occasions, and leaves his creation's dealings with him in the hand of purblind and clumsy amateurs" (55), which is what we all are. The "shabby occasion" she speaks of is the weekly church service—the one she attends, and many others. She says:

> [N]othing could more surely convince me of God's unending mercy than the continued existence on earth of the church. The higher Christian churches—where, if anywhere, I belong—come at God with an unwarranted air of professionalism, with authority and pomp, as though they knew what they were doing, as though people in themselves were an appropriate set of creatures to have dealings with God. I often think of the set pieces of the liturgy as certain words which people have successfully addressed to God without their getting killed. In the high churches they saunter through the liturgy like Mohawks along a strand of scaffolding who

have long since forgotten their danger. If God were to blast such a service to bits, the congregation would be, I believe, genuinely shocked. But in the low churches you expect it any minute. This is the beginning of wisdom. (59)

I quote this lengthy passage to illumine not so much what Dillard has to say about church services, but about the kind of God that is invoked during them.[1] The model of God that she proposes here—that of a God that might "blow a service to bits"— is not the model most likely to come to the minds of those who think of God in terms of love, caring, healing, liberation, and justice. Granted, Dillard is not, in this specific passage, talking about nature and deriving her model of God from nature; this model of a God who might blow a service to bits, however, is entirely consistent with the conception of God she purports in *Pilgrim*, a model based almost entirely upon the natural world. In fact, the model she presents here in the church passage can be said to be an extension of the model advanced in *Pilgrim*. This passage, then, is one more illustration of the holy and dangerous God that Dillard deduces from her look at nature, except that, here, this God is placed in the context of church.

Dillard leaves the subject of church and returns to burned Julie Norwich. She notes that burn victims have a high suicide rate because "they had not realized, before they were burned, that life could include such suffering, nor that they personally could be permitted such pain" (60). Without a transition, Dillard quotes from the New Testament the passage in which the disciples, upon seeing a blind man, ask Jesus who sinned, the blind man or his parents, that he was born blind. Jesus answers that neither sinned, but that the man is blind so that the works of God would be manifested. Dillard responds:

> Really? If we take this answer to refer to the affliction itself—and not the subsequent cure—as "God's works made manifest," then we have, along with "Not as the world gives do I give unto you," two meager, baffling and infuriating answers to one of the few questions worth asking, to wit, What in the Sam Hill is going on here? The works of God made manifest? Do we really need more victims to remind us that we're all victims? Is this some sort of parade for which a conquering army shines up its terrible guns and rolls them up and down the streets for the people to see? Do we need blind men stumbling about, and little flame-faced children, to remind is what God can—and will—do? (60–1)

Dillard's exasperation is evident here as she identifies God as a victimizer. God victimizes in that the world that s/he has provided is one that remains irrevocably subject to the conditions of time and freedom, which include always the possibility of danger (as well as beauty and safety) and the inevitability of death. Readers might expect Dillard to answer her last few rhetorical questions posed above in the negative. She, however, answers in the affirmative:

Yes, in fact, we do. We do need reminding, not of what God can do, but of what he cannot do, or will not, which is to catch time in its free fall and stick a nickel's worth of sense into our days. And we need reminding of what time can do, must only do; churn out enormity at random and beat it, with God's blessing, into our heads: that we are created, *created*, sojourners in a land we did not make ... Who are we to demand explanations from God? (And what monsters of perfection should we be if we did not?) We forget ourselves, picnicking; we forget where we are. There is no such thing as a freak accident. "God is at home," says Meister Eckhart, "We are in the far country." We are most deeply asleep at the switches when we fancy we control any switches at all. (61–2)

It is because of the conditions of human existence in the world—conditions which have God's full blessing—that people suffer what they like to call "freak accidents." In truth, there is no freak accident, because such accidents are inevitable given the conditions of time, space, matter, and freedom. What those conditions testify to, in Dillard's view, is the enormity of the landscape of the universe and, more importantly, the tiny dot that is a single human life in the context of that landscape. This is not to dismiss the earnestness with which we humans live our lives—with which Dillard lives her own life—but to soberly maintain that earnestness, love, faith, *nothing* stops the churning wheel of time that brings random occasions of peace and violence, mercy and tragedy into our lives. When we forget the conditions under which we live—"picnicking," as Dillard says—when we forget that the world is not an anthropocentric one, and that to live in this world means having to die at its hands, one way or another, then we deceive ourselves most surely, and are fast asleep. These are not new themes for Dillard. She introduced them at length in *Pilgrim* and continues them here, in *Teaching a Stone to Talk* and in her novel, *The Living*. I will discuss these themes yet again as the chapter progresses.[2]

Although God has abandoned the world to time, it is not true that God does not "have a stake" in the world. Dillard, at the end of *Holy the Firm*, waxes mystical as she speaks of the substance called Holy the Firm, a substance posited by esoteric Christianity to account for the relationship between God and matter. Holy the Firm is "a created substance, lower than metals and minerals on the 'spiritual scale,' and lower than salts and earths ... in the waxy deepness of planets ... and it is in touch with the Absolute, at base" (68–9). Since Holy the Firm is in touch with the Absolute at base, and Holy the Firm is at the deepest part of the planet and must, therefore, seep into earth's plants, waters, and rocks, then the earth is connected to the Absolute at both ends, and "the circle is unbroken" (70). The world emanates from God, yet, in its deepest core, remains in touch with the Absolute no matter how remote the diffusion. This piece of mystical, Neoplatonist, Christianity serves Dillard as a metaphor by which she can conceive of the world as reflecting the divine, even though its conditions are toothed and clawed, and even though such a conception necessitates that she envision God as toothed and clawed as well.

At the very end of the third section, which is also the end of the book, Dillard returns to the image of burned Julie Norwich, whom she describes as being "baptized now into time and now into eternity, into the bladelike arms of God" (73). Julie has been baptized into the world, inducted into the "way things are" in the world, initiated into holy mysteries. Dillard spends several pages comparing Julie to a nun, and the burned flesh of her face to a veil. She encourages Julie to learn Latin, sing praises, and, most importantly, "learn power, however sweet they call you, learn power, the smash of the holy once more, and signed by his name" (75). The language is important here. Dillard refers to the "smash" of the holy, rather than the caress or healing touch. Julie is to learn this smash "once more" because she has already learned it once, having been burned in a "freak accident." In these passages, Dillard unites the images of the burning moth acting as a wick in the flame with the burned Julie Norwich and the saintliness and devotion to God of the historic figure who is evoked by Julie's name, that is, Julian of Norwich. As the moth is attracted to the flame that takes its life, and transforms its body into something else, so the saint is drawn to the God who takes her life, burns her face—as if she were Moses on the mountaintop—and alters her life so that she lives transfigured by fire. Here, the lines between oppressive violence and a visitation from the holy blur. The God who "smashes" and who is likely to "blast" church services to bits is not to be avoided; quite the contrary, s/he is to be sought out in whatever dangerous places s/he may reside, stalked like the muskrats and fish in *Pilgrim*, pursued relentlessly without sleep or sustenance, if necessary, just for the experience of being smashed or burned by the really real, the Absolute. Dillard's is a daredevil spirituality, one not comforted by notions of a God who deals only in life, nurturance, and healing. Again, this God is seen—and paradoxically, *not* seen, but hidden—in nature, in the givens of the universe.

Holy the Firm, then, explicates further the themes introduced in *Pilgrim*, themes that have to do with the presence of God in nature, the ecstasy of submitting to that presence, and the violence incurred in that submission. A very distinct image of God emerges from these texts, an image that does not rely so much upon scriptural sentiments of security, promise, redemption, healing, and salvation. Using the natural, given world as her sacred text, Dillard interprets from its pages a God of great power, mysterious intention, majestic splendor, and utter impartiality in dealing with the various entities in the creation. The setting of the book—Puget Sound— serves Dillard well in her explication of the theological ideas she deduces from her observations of nature, so well that she chooses the Pacific Northwest again as the setting for a few of the essays in *Teaching a Stone to Talk*, and for *The Living*. As will soon be seen, the setting is not the only familiar feature to any reader of Dillard.

Purity, Risk, and the Negation of the Self

Teaching a Stone to Talk: Expeditions and Encounters is a collection of fourteen essays, seven of which I will discuss here, some in greater depth than others. The essay most important for my argument is "An Expedition to the Pole," in which Dillard masterfully interweaves facts about nineteenth-century polar explorers, her experiences attending a Catholic church, and thoughts about the nature of God. The essay is written in first person narrative, and begins with Dillard's comments on a singing group that has come to perform at the Catholic church she attends. She thinks the group is out of place in the Catholic setting, but admits that, in spite of this, they and she and all others have "access to the land" (18). By this she means that all people everywhere have access to the divine, to the spiritual journey; in typical Dillardian fashion, the divine here is associated with the material, the land. The next small section of the essay is titled "The Land," in which she speaks of the Pole of Relative Inaccessibility, "that imaginary point on the Arctic Ocean farthest from any land in any direction," or, in Antarctica, "that point of land farthest from salt water in any direction" (18). In the very next sentence, she identifies the Absolute, or God, with the Pole of Relative Inaccessibility in metaphysics. "After all," she says, "one of the few things we know about the Absolute is that it is relatively inaccessible. It is that point of spirit farthest from every accessible point of spirit in all directions" (19). So, here she firms the analogy between the material Poles and the spiritual Absolute, and prepares the reader for an essay about polar exploration which is a metaphor for spiritual quest. She concludes this small section on "The Land" by saying that the Absolute is the "Pole of the Most Trouble. It is also—I take this as given—the pole of great price" (19). This statement is a re-statement, if the reader has read either *Pilgrim* or *Holy the Firm*, of Dillard's commitment to stalking the divine regardless of the cognitive, psychological, or physical costs.

In the next section, entitled "The People," Dillard describes the Catholic church service in much the same way that she described the Congregationalist service in *Holy the Firm*. She notes the amateurish quality of the proceedings, the propensity for error and the general "humanness" of the whole event. After comparing the church service to a circus and parishioners to dancing bears, she says:

> A high school play is more polished than this service we have been rehearsing since the year one. In two thousand years, we have not worked out the kinks. We positively glorify them. Week after week we witness the same miracle: that God is so mighty he can stifle his own laughter. Week after week, we witness the same miracle: that God, for reasons unfathomable, refrains from blowing our dancing bear act to smithereens. Week after week Christ washes the disciples' dirty feet, handles their very toes, and repeats, It is all right—believe it or not—to be people. Who can believe it? (20)

Here, Dillard speaks as she does in *Holy the Firm*, albeit in a lighter tone, of God as a power able to "blow people away," especially those who gather to seek or serve him. From this assertion, she shifts her narrative to a discussion of the nineteenth century polar explorers and the difficulty involved in their quest for the Pole. What might normally seem like an abrupt change of subject—from the quest for God to the various expeditions to the Pole—is quite the opposite, for Dillard speaks of the spiritual quest *as* she speaks of the material one, so that the two are reflective of each other. Therefore, the hardships of one are analogous to those of the other; likewise, the ecstasy of one is analogous to that of the other.

Of Dillard's descriptions of the polar expeditions, one of the most detailed is her summary of the Franklin expedition of 1845, of which there were no survivors. The main reason given for the failure of the expedition and the death of the men is that, rather than travelling with equipment and supplies adapted to the harsh conditions of the Canadian Arctic, their outfit "was adapted only to conditions in the Royal Navy officers' clubs in England" (24). Instead of Arctic necessities like coal, thick clothing, light gear, and carefully planned eating arrangements, the Franklin expedition hauled with them a 1,200 volume library, an organ, expensive china, silver flatware and goblets, only a 12-day supply of coal, and no heavy parkas, only their Navy uniforms. Their bodies and skeletons were discovered for the next twenty years, often in possession of the ornate flatware or china they had insisted upon retaining for their journey. Another explorer, Sir Robert Falcon Scott, died in the Antarctic because he was not willing to use dogs and opted, instead, for English ponies for whom he carried bales of hay. He considered it inhumane to use dogs and to do as successful explorers later did, which was to use dogs not only to pull sleds, but also to feed them to each other on a schedule and, sometimes, to eat them themselves. These later, successful expeditions were "'adapted to harsh conditions'" (27), and threw aside their notions of dignity and humaneness, which were out of context in the Arctic. They were keenly aware of the conditions in which they travelled and knew of the likelihood of their death. Polar explorers, Dillard recounts, suffered and/or died of starvation, drowning, scurvy, dysentery, bleeding gums, frostbite, and mental confusion, among other things. Those who knew of these possibilities beforehand, and prepared for them, were obviously most likely to succeed.

From this account of various polar expeditions, Dillard shifts to another short section entitled "The Land," in which she talks about God and life with God, again making the familiar association of divinity with the material, natural world. She says:

> God does not demand that we give up our personal dignity, that we throw in our lot with random people, that we lose ourselves and turn from all that is not him. God needs nothing, asks nothing, and demands nothing, like the stars. It is life with God which demands these things. . . . You do not have to do these things; not at all. God does not, I regret to report, give a hoot. You do not have to do these things—unless you want to know God. They work on you, not on him. You do not have to sit outside in the dark. If, however, you want to look at the stars, you will find that darkness is necessary. But the stars neither require it nor demand it. (31)

This passage reasserts that God is like the Pole, in that neither, in themselves, require that those who seek them give up their ornate silver flatware, or eat dogmeat, or relinquish their fine uniforms, or cast aside notions of what is and what is not humane. God and the Pole are unaffected by these things; however, if one wants to reach the Pole or God, one has to do these things, for they are supremely adapted to the conditions, respectively. Dillard pushes further this comparison between the expedition to the Pole and the quest for God when she complains of having to sing the Sanctus with the extremely folksy singing group at her Catholic church. She would rather chant it, or sing it in Latin. She says:

> Must I join this song? May I keep only my silver? My backgammon board, I agree, is a frivolity. I relinquish it. I will leave it right here on the ice. But my silver? My family crest? One knife, one fork, one spoon, to carry beneath the glance of heaven and back . . . [b]ut these purely personal preferences are of no account, and maladaptive to boot. They are passing the plate and I toss in my schooling; I toss in my rank in the Royal Navy, my erroneous and incomplete charts, my pious refusal to eat sled dogs, my watch, my keys, and my shoes . . . who can argue with conditions? (33)

This passage, additionally, illustrates the spiritual posture Dillard takes in reference to the Absolute, an anti-rationalistic posture characterized by emptiness brought on by a relinquishing of preconceived ideas about God, lofty notions of the worthiness and dignity of oneself, and predetermined and purely personal goals one might have had in seeking the divine. To do otherwise would be not only presumptuous, but naive and unmindful of conditions.

On this note, Dillard later asks, "Why do we people in churches seem like cheerful, brainless tourists on a packaged tour of the Absolute?" (40). This question is reminiscent of the passage in *Holy the Firm* in which she says the liturgy is a collection of words people have said to God without being killed. Both passages assume a God that is terribly powerful, and deeply deserving of respect and even dread on the part of those who would seek him/her. Dillard continues in this vein, and pushes even further the comparison between the spiritual quest and the polar expeditions, God and the Pole:

> On the whole, I do not find Christians, outside of the catacombs, sufficiently sensible of conditions. Does anyone have the foggiest idea what sort of power we so blithely invoke? Or, as I suspect, does no one believe a word of it? The churches are children playing on the floor with their chemistry sets, mixing up a batch of TNT to kill a Sunday morning. It is madness to wear ladies' straw hats and velvet hats to church; we should all be wearing crash helmets. Ushers should issue life preservers and signal flares; they should lash us to our pews. For the sleeping god may wake someday and take offense, or the waking god may draw us out to where we can never return. (40–1)

This passage and others like it serve as a critique to all versions of religion, all exercises in theology that envision a God who is, so to speak, at their service.

Those theologies which "blithely invoke" the power of God to buttress their own goals—personal, political, social, economic or otherwise—are, in Dillard's estimation, utterly oblivious to the kind of God that is evidenced by the realities in the natural world. Were they truly mindful of these realities—"sufficiently sensible of conditions"—they would know that they, like the polar explorers, must relinquish such goals at the outset of the journey, set aside their rational notions of goodness or justice, and realize the non-anthropocentric character of the divine power they seek. In Dillard's view, eighteenth-century Hasidic Jews "had more sense and more belief" (41). She tells of two such persons:

> One Hasidic slaughterer, whose work required invoking the Lord, bade a tearful farewell to his wife and children every morning before he set out for the slaughterhouse. He felt, every morning, that he would never see any of them again. For every day, as he himself stood with his knife in his hand, the words of his prayer carried him into danger. After he called on God, God might notice and destroy him before he had time to utter the rest, "Have mercy." Another Hasid, a rabbi, refused to promise a friend to visit him the next day: "How can you ask me to make such a promise? This evening I must pray and recite 'Hear, O Israel.' When I say these words, my soul goes out to the utmost rim of life . . . .Perhaps I shall not die this time either, but how can I promise to do something at a time after the prayer?" (41)[3]

The beauty of these Hasidim for Dillard is that they have a keen and accurate image of the kind of God they worship. They know what she herself asserts in *Holy the Firm*, namely, that all prayers are rash because they by definition bring the one praying into the presence of a holy and utterly deadly God. The Hasidim here, like the Christians whose bodies lie in the catacombs, are truly mindful of the conditions of the divine, conditions which are mirrored in nature. For example, Dillard mentions Lieutenant Maxwell of the Vitus Bering expedition, who wrote, "'You never feel safe when you have to navigate in waters which are completely blank'" (47). The blank waters here are a metaphor for God. The blank waters may indicate peaceful currents and safe passage, or they may conceal deadly rocks and reefs; likewise, the "blank face" of God may manifest a lack of malice and a tendency toward mercy, or it may conceal a fatal indifference and want of concern for human life.

    In the end, Dillard collapses her account of the Catholic church service and her summaries of the various polar expeditions into one narrative, so that she imagines herself and all the others at the church—the priests, the folksy singing group, the other parishioners, even Christ—as floating together on an ice floe, having been joined by several polar expedition members. Some are more concerned about "conditions" than others; therefore, while some juggle, play the piano, and pose for snapshots, others measure the ice floe, and look toward the horizon for bearings. Some have even staked themselves to the ice floe with tent stakes and ropes. Readers are reminded here of the one of the concluding images in *Pilgrim*, that of Dillard staked at the wrists and ankles to the bloodstained rock altar of the world, an act of self-sacrifice to given, natural realities, and the deity present in them. Those staked here on the ice floe are not on rock, granted, but their ice altar is no less bloodstained, splattered as it is in the blood and bones of those many explorers who died trying to reach the sublime they surmised to be at the Pole. Concerning the quest that is represented in this essay in terms both physical and metaphysical, Dillard says:

> I have a taste for solitude, and silence, and for what Plotinus called "the flight of the alone to the Alone." . . . You quit your house and country, quit your ship, and quit your companions in the tent . . . the light on the far side of the blizzard lures you. You walk, and one day you enter the spread heart of silence, where lands dissolve and seas become vapor and ice sublime under unknown stars. This is the end of the Via Negativa, the lightless edge where the slopes of knowledge dwindle, and love for its own sake begins. (48)

The journey to the Pole, this "northing" as she calls it in *Pilgrim*, is another example of the posture of passivity mentioned earlier in the chapter, a stance toward the divine and/or the natural given that involves being played upon, dabbled with, and even blasted. Lured by the light of experience with God, one leaves everything familiar and submits to whatever is necessary in order to attain that experience. Here, the concept of *via negativa* defines not only an approach to the doctrine of God that defines deity by what it is not, rather than what it is; *via negativa* here refers also to the negative or negating aspects of life in quest for the divine. Here, on the 'negative way', the self is negated: staked to an altar of ice waiting for the knife of the wind or the cold; lodged upright and burning in a stand of wax, like the moth of *Holy the Firm* that tropes burned Julie Norwich and mystic Julian of Norwich; tied to the altar of the world in *Pilgrim* waiting for worms, grasshoppers or locusts to begin eating at the wrists and throat—all this in order to experience the really real, the given, the Absolute, deity.

Dillard explicates such passivity—which, paradoxically, obtains in the midst of quite deliberate activities, such as stalking—in several of the essays in *Teaching*, but specifically in two, entitled "Total Eclipse" and "Living Like Weasels" respectively. "Total Eclipse" is the story of Dillard and her husband, who journeyed to an area of Washington State in order to "put [themselves] in the path of [a] total eclipse" (85). This "putting oneself in the path" is reminiscent of Dillard's goal in *Pilgrim*, which was to put herself in the path of spirit, wherever it may manifest itself in nature. Readers get a sense of dread and impending danger when Dillard recounts that, as they neared the high altitude from which to view the eclipse, she "watched the landscape innocently, like a fool, like a diver in the rapture of the deep who plays on the bottom while his air runs out" (86). She notes that in the lobby of the hotel where she stayed, she glanced at a magazine article about gold mining, and learned that certain gold mines are so deep that mining companies have to air condition the mines to keep the miners alive during their work. Furthermore, the elevators have to run very slowly, to and from the surface, to keep the miner's ears from exploding. "When the miners return to the surface," she says, "their faces are deathly pale" (87). This short account of gold mining occurs early in the essay, and is an indicator that the essay will have to do with encountering the natural world in one of its extreme moments. As I have argued, encountering the natural world, for Dillard, is synonymous with encountering God, whether it is the shadow of the moon during an eclipse, or the deadly heat of the shafts in a gold mine.

What began for Dillard as a pleasant experience—watching the sky turn increasingly deeper shades of blue, the towns below come into sharper relief—turned into a terrifying experience in which Dillard experienced herself, her husband, and all others on the hill with them as being transported to the realm of the dead. As the sun disappeared behind the moon, all the colors faded from the world, the sky was dark blue and all else was a metallic color that reminded Dillard of an old photograph. The familiar face of her husband took on age and death in the platinum light, and as the last piece of the sun disappeared and dark night descended upon them, "[f]rom all the hills came screams" (92). Dillard continues:

> There was no sound. The eyes dried, the arteries drained, the lungs hushed. There was no world. We were the world's dead people rotating and orbiting around and around, embedded in the planet's crust, while the earth rolled down. Our minds were light-years distant, forgetful of almost everything. Only an extraordinary act of will could recall us to our former, living selves and our contexts in matter and time. We had, it seems, loved the planet and loved our lives, but could no longer remember the way of them. (93)

Immediately following this passage of the essay, Dillard evokes the image of the gold mine:

> It is now that the temptation is strongest to leave these regions. We have seen enough; let's go. Why burn our hands any more than we have to? But two years have passed; the price of gold has risen. I return to the same buried alluvial beds and pick through the strata again. (93)

Drawing the analogy between the gold mine and the experience of the eclipse emphasizes the importance of death in both instances. In the mine, one is, every minute, on the verge of actual death. On the hill, watching the eclipse, Dillard felt as though she were dead, got to envision herself, her husband, and the world as if they were dead; furthermore, she got a taste of her own impermanence, the relative nature of her own life and concerns in relation to all other lives and concerns throughout the ages. In both instances, death—either actual or virtual—is the risk taken for attaining what one comes for in the first place: gold or a view of the eclipse. In order to acquire gold or a view of the eclipse, one has to put oneself in their paths, which involves, quite possibly, death.

Later, in a restaurant which Dillard labels "a decompression chamber" (100), she reflects on the event and determines that, rather than the sudden darkness brought on by the eclipse, it was, in fact, the racing shadow of the moon that had made everyone on the hill scream. She says:

> The second before the sun went out we saw a wall of dark shadow come speeding at us. We no sooner saw it than it was upon us, like thunder. It roared up the valley. It slammed our hill and knocked us out. It was the monstrous swift shadow cone of the moon . . . [moving] 1800 miles an hour. Language can give no sense of this sort of speed. . . . It was 195 miles wide . . . It rolled at you across the land at 1,800 miles an hour, hauling darkness like a plague behind it. . . . We saw the wall of shadow coming, and screamed before it hit. This was the universe about which we have read so much and never before felt: the universe as a clockwork of loose spheres flung at stupefying, unauthorized speeds. . . . Less than two minutes later, when the sun emerged, the trailing edge of the shadow cone sped away. It coursed down our hill and raced eastward over the plain, faster than the eye could believe; it swept over the plain and dropped over the planet's rim in a twinkling. It had clobbered us, and now it roared away. We blinked in the light. It was as though an enormous, loping god in the sky had reached down and slapped the earth's face. (100–1)

For Dillard, God, in all his/her enormity and death-wielding power, has come in the eclipse and slapped her in the face. I quote at length from this passage in order to give the fullest possible meaning to the last sentence of the quote. God here appears not as light, but as shadow that not only casts a foreign tint on all that is familiar, but "clobbers" all with the magnitude of its own reality over against that of those who dare to watch. Furthermore, the one who dares to watch, in doing so, submits herself to the force of this loping god, allowing herself to experience virtual death as a result of placing herself within its very path. This is the posture of passivity that Dillard promotes throughout most of her work.

Surprisingly—or perhaps not—Dillard, at the end of the essay, refers to the event of the eclipse as a "glory." Speaking of the haste with which she and all the others left the hills after the eclipse, she says:

> We never looked back. It was a general vamoose, and an odd one, for when we left the hill, the sun was still partially eclipsed—a sight rare enough, and one which, in itself, we would probably have driven five hours to see. But enough is enough. One turns at last even from glory itself with a sigh of relief. From the depths of mystery, and even from the heights of splendor, we bounce back and hurry for the latitudes of home. (103)

The "depths of mystery" and the "heights of splendor" here can refer to the depths of the mine shafts and the heights of the hills on which they stood to view the eclipse. Although these depths and heights are terrifying and deadly, Dillard still refers to them with words such as "glory," "mystery," and "splendor." For her, any glance at the really real, the Absolute, or the naturally given is an occasion of glory and splendor, even as it requires her own negation—a posture of passivity—and forces her to realize the inevitability of her own death, the tenuousness of her existence, and her relativity in the world.

Dillard's passive stance toward the Absolute is illustrated most clearly in the opening essay of the *Teaching* collection, entitled "Living Like Weasels." The essay is inspired by a chance meeting with a weasel Dillard had while sitting beside a pond. After the encounter she began to read about weasels, and learned of their tenacity and obedience to instinct. She tells of a naturalist who "refused to kill a weasel who was socketed into his hand deeply as a rattlesnake. The man could in no way pry the tiny weasel off, and he had to walk half a mile to water, the weasel dangling from his palm, and soak him off like a stubborn label" (11). Another story tells of a man who shot an eagle and, upon examining the eagle,

> found the dry skull of a weasel fixed by the jaws to his throat. The supposition is that the eagle had pounced on the weasel and the weasel swiveled and bit as instinct taught him, tooth to neck, and nearly won. I would like to have seen that eagle from the air a few weeks or months before he was shot: was the whole weasel still attached to his throat like a fur pendant? Or did the eagle eat what he could reach, gutting the living weasel with his talons before his breast, bending his neck, cleaning the beautiful airborne bones? (12)

The dominant image in both these stories is of the fierce and determined weasel refusing to loose its hold on whatever it had seized, submitting itself to whatever fate that hold might bring to it, whether it be a meal, injury, death, or all three. The image here is an important one, for Dillard has this image in mind when she states toward the middle of the essay that from the weasel she "would like to learn, or remember, how to live" (15). She suggests that, from the weasel, she "might learn something of mindlessness, something of the purity of living in the physical senses and the dignity of living without bias or motive" (15). She goes on to say that in order to live as she should, she should live like the weasel: "open to time and death painlessly, noticing everything, remembering nothing, choosing the given with a fierce and pointed will" (15). Her description of the weasel here resembles her description of the monk on the road at the end of *Pilgrim*, the monk who "walk[s] fearlessly, eating what [he] must . . . who knows precisely how vulnerable he is, who takes no comfort among death-forgetting men . . . " (270). The monk, like the weasel, has made peace with the given, with the irrefutable conditions of his life in this world. Both illustrate, for Dillard, a kind of living that is pure, full of dignity, and truly spiritual.

At the end of the essay, the image of the weasel motivates Dillard to encourage her readers to "stalk your calling in a certain skilled and supple way, to locate the most tender and live spot and plug into that pulse. This is yielding, not fighting . . . yielding at every moment to the perfect freedom of a single necessity" (16). The verb "stalk" here, of course, evokes the chapter in *Pilgrim* devoted entirely to stalking muskrats, fish, and, ultimately, God. Clearly, Dillard is talking about the spiritual life and deity, even as she speaks about weasels. The essay ends with a sort of charge that Dillard issues, bearing in mind the images of the weasel hanging from the naturalist's hand and from the eagle's breast, being lifted and gutted. In this charge, the passivity before deity that has become characteristic of the spiritual life for Dillard is keenly apparent. She says:

> I think it would be well, and proper, and obedient, and pure, to grasp your one necessity and not let it go, to dangle from it limp wherever it takes you. Then even death, where you're going no matter how you live, cannot you part. Seize it and let it seize you up aloft even, till your eyes burn out and drop; let your musky flesh fall off in shreds, and let your very bones unhinge and scatter, loosened over fields, over fields and woods, lightly, thoughtless, from any height at all, from as high as eagles. (16)

Dillard's one necessity has, hopefully, become apparent: experience with God, unshielded confrontation with the given. Here, the weasel becomes a metaphor for the self that is put at risk in pursuit of and in the presence of deity. Furthermore, this passivity, this letting oneself be seized and dispersed by the deity is reified as a pure, obedient, and true way to live.[4] This entire passage runs parallel thematically to the passage in the last part of *Pilgrim*, in which Dillard speaks of stalking the gaps, going into the clifts of mountains to see God, and coming back transformed and crazed, even cognitively ravaged. Of course, all this assumes a certain kind of deity, a deity of power and vastness, a deity not to be tinkered with, a deity who is "not playful" (Dillard 1974, 270), and, more importantly, a deity whose mysterious and unfathomable concerns often bypass and confound our own.

Two essays in *Teaching* that speak to the mysterious ways of deity are the title essay of the volume, "Teaching a Stone to Talk," and "A Field of Silence." In the former Dillard begins by mentioning Larry, a man living nearby who is trying to teach a stone how to talk. She says she and others who live in the area respect Larry for what he is trying to do. Readers quickly learn that the stone represents nature, and the voice that would come from it, if it ever spoke, would be the voice of God. This essay, then, is about the silence of God, about how, if God is to be heard at all, it will be through nature. She laments that "[w]e as a people have moved from pantheism to pan-atheism," in that we have driven the divinity from its "sacred groves" and "snuffed it in the high places and along the banks of sacred streams" (69). We have done, in short, what the Israelites did when they asked Moses to ask God never to speak to them again, for when they saw and heard God on the mountaintop—"the thunderings, and the lightnings, and the noise of the trumpet, and the mountain smoking" (69)—they were afraid. God agreed never to speak to them again and told them to return to their tents. Now, Dillard maintains:

> What have we been trying to do all these centuries but trying to call God back to the mountain, or, failing that, raise a peep out of anything that isn't us? What is the difference between a cathedral and a physics lab? Are they not both saying: Hello? We spy on whales and on interstellar radio objects; we starve ourselves and pray till we're blue. (71)

The silence of God is "all there is" (72), and the most that we can do, "[u]ntil Larry teaches his stone to talk, until God changes his mind" (72), is to simply watch, so that when birds sing, or whales surface, or waves break, we may hear "the still small voice, God's speaking from the whirlwind, nature's old song and dance, the show we drove from town" (70). This is familiar territory; Dillard named 'seeing' as her methodology for learning about God from the beginning of *Pilgrim*. Her emphasis on silence here, though, is an indication of the mysteriousness of God: God's ways are mysterious because of God's silence. To declare with any certainty God's allegiance with any human objective is to be presumptuous, and to speak too soon. Dillard concludes the essay:

> The silence is all there is. It is the alpha and the omega. It is God's brooding over the face of the waters; it is the blended note of ten thousand things, the whine of wings. You take a step in the right direction to pray to this silence, and even to address the prayer to "World." Distinctions blur. Quit your tents. Pray without ceasing. (76)

Again, the conflation of God and world here is expected. The exhortation to "quit your tents" is reminiscent not only of the polar explorer who "quit[s] [his] companions in the tent" (48) to follow the light on the far side of the blizzard—leaving the familiar for the unknown—but also recalls the tents of the Israelites in which they stayed to escape the voice of God. Dillard's injunction here to "quit your tents" is, in effect, an injunction to submit oneself to the voice of God, which remains terrifying even though mediated and quiesced, as it is, through nature.

Dillard's thoughts on silence continue in "A Field of Silence," an essay about an epiphany she had while staring at the hayfields of a farm where she once lived. She calls the day on which this happened a "God-blasted, paralyzed day" (136). She had simply come out of the house, sat on a wooden fence beside a crowing rooster and looked out at the fields. Suddenly, she says:

I saw silence heaped on the fields like trays. That day the green hayfields supported silence evenly sown; the fields bent just so under the even pressure of silence, bearing it, palming it aloft. . . . I do not want, I think, ever to see such a sight again. That there is loneliness here I had granted, in the abstract—but not, I thought, inside the light of God's presence, inside his sanction, and signed by his name. (133–4)

The experience of silence here, then, is an unpleasant one, one that speaks of profound loneliness and isolation. She goes on:

I had to try to turn away. Holiness is a force, and like the others can be resisted. It was given, but I didn't want to see it, God or no God. It was as if God had said, "I am here, but not as you have known me. This is the look of silence, and of loneliness unendurable; it too has always been mine, and now will be yours." I was not ready for a life of sorrow, sorrow deriving from knowledge I could just as well stop at the gate. I turned away, willful, and the whole show vanished. (136–7)

Just as she made a hasty retreat from the hill of the total eclipse, so she stops this vision of silence in its tracks when she can no longer bear it. Bear what? A profound experience with deity that illumined, more powerfully than ever before, the realities of silence and loneliness. The epiphany here is an experience with deity on the 'negative way', an experience that leaves her scarred, shaken, and changed, and that contrasts sharply with other, more common, accounts of epiphany that focus on love, union, and/or peace.

The point I want to make about these meditations on silence is that the deity that lurks behind them is one that is not represented by the comforting, nurturing models of deity proposed by much political theology in America. This obtains despite the fact that both Dillard and many of these theologians, especially those whose work is typified by McFague's, derive their models, in some degree, from nature. The deity Dillard envisions is one who, while perhaps having a propensity for loving, nurturing, and healing, is revealed most clearly in nature to be impartial, vast in an often terrifying way, a harborer of deadly force and mysterious intention, and reconciled to the fact that everything and everyone dies, sometimes without warning and often violently and tragically.

Two more essays from *Teaching* deserve treatment here, and both center around what I call the sojourner motif in Dillard's work, a motif that later becomes excruciatingly apparent in her novel, *The Living*. The first, "Life on the Rocks: The Galapagos," obviously, tells of Dillard's experiences and observations of the Galapagos Islands; however, the phrase "on the rocks" becomes descriptive of the condition of the human life in the world. The dominant image is of the human life as perched precariously among the rocks that are the natural world (remember the "bloodstained rock altar of the world"), alternately thriving on and barely surviving the rough edges. When Dillard states early in the essay that "[b]eing here is being on the rocks" (111), she is not only speaking specifically of the Galapagos; she is speaking for the world at large. While it is entirely possible for life to flourish in a myriad of dazzling ways—as the species on the Galapagos islands prove—it is also a given that life on such rough terrain can be brutal.

After spending several pages describing various species of animals on the islands, Dillard begins a new paragraph with:

> We are strangers and sojourners, soft dots in the rocks. You have walked along the strand and seen where birds have landed, walked, and flown; their tracks begin in sand, and go, and suddenly end. Our tracks do that; but we go down. And stay down. (115)

She evokes the passage from the Psalms which speaks of humans as being strangers before God; here, however, the rocks supplant God as being the entity before whom we are sojourners and strangers. Of course, it is quite possible to equate divinity and rocks in Dillard's scheme. Moreover, Dillard turns her observation about humans being "soft dots on the rocks" to a comment about death. That we as humans are precisely soft dots on the rocks implies that we die there on those same rocks, our flesh being not so hard as to protect us from their edges, and then go down to our earthen graves under the rocks. The rocks ultimately win, since everything dies, except the rocks. "Life" and "the rocks," often incompatible, are nevertheless intertwined: "[l]ife and the rocks, like spirit and matter, are a fringed matrix, lapped and lapping, clasping and held. It is like hand washing hand . . . and the whole tumult hurled" (130). "Life" and "the rocks" are a fringed matrix in the same way that beauty and horror are in *Pilgrim*; in fact, the two sets of metaphors refer to the same reality, the same "guarantee" of life in this world: that in order to live you have to die. "The rocks," Dillard's metaphor for the world, are like the rocks of the Galapagos: they are "home to a[n] . . . assortment of windblown, stowaway, castaway, flotsam, and shipwrecked creatures" (112). We, as humans, are no less such creatures than the iguanas or the blue-footed booby. Dillard here reiterates the point she made in the "Fecundity" chapter of *Pilgrim*, namely, that "the sea is a cup of death and the land is a stained altar stone. We the living are survivors huddled on flotsam, living on jetsam. We are escapees. We wake in terror, eat in hunger, sleep with a mouthful of blood" (Dillard 1974, 174–5).

Dillard supplements the above view with an assertion of relativity concerning the planet Earth and our activities upon it. Visiting the Galapagos has emphasized, for Dillard, the changing landscape of the planet over eons, from which Dillard extrapolates the place the planet has in the larger context of our solar system, and, even further, the standing our solar system has among the millions of others. The human life—an entire civilization, for that matter—becomes tiny when placed into the context of the vast landscape that is the universe. "The planet spins, rapt in its intricate mists. The galaxy is a flung thing, loose in the night, and our solar system is one of many dotted campfires ringed with tossed rocks. What shall we sing?" (130) It is just this vision of vastness that drives the models of deity in Dillard's work in the direction of sovereignty. By this I mean that God, metaphorized by the natural world and/or the universe, takes on, literally, larger than life proportions so that s/he becomes sovereign, *not* in the strictly Calvinist sense that God predestines all events in all places and times, but in the acknowledgment that the universe is utterly *theocentric*: that taken against the expansive backdrop that is the world, human concerns, will, needs, and desires are hardly prioritized no matter how keenly they are felt or expressed on the individual level.

I borrow the term 'theocentric' from James Gustafson, whose *Ethics from a Theocentric Perspective* speaks of God in a way that strongly resembles the image of deity I argue for here. When Gustafson says that the universe is theocentric, he asserts the sovereignty of the power in the universe, which he labels 'God'; he highlights "the power and powers man did not and cannot create, powers that sustain and bear down on us as well as create possibilities for human achievement" (vol. 2, 321). In his estimation,

> Ethics in theocentric perspective does not guarantee happiness . . . It requires consenting to the governance of the powers of God, and joining in those powers that can be discerned. God does not exist simply for the service of man; man exists for the service of God." (Gustafson 1981, 1:342)

Gustafson writes from within a Reformed Calvinist tradition and is, naturally, highly informed by the theology of Jonathan Edwards, specifically on issues of divine sovereignty and governance. What is explicitly Calvinistic in Gustafson is implicitly so in Dillard; her notions of sovereignty and theocentrism, however, are discerned not primarily in theological or biblical assertions about God, but in what sober observation of the natural world tells her about deity.

The final essay from *Teaching* that I want to treat here is entitled "Sojourner" and considers the plight of mangroves, "short, messy trees, waxy-leaved, laced all over with aerial roots, woody arching buttresses, and weird leathery berry pods. All this tangles from a black muck soil, a black muck matted like a mud-sopped rag . . . " (148). Mangroves are created when a hurricane or tide rips a tree from its home on the shore and casts it out to sea. If the tree brings soil with it to the ocean, it has a better chance of staying alive; otherwise it has to manufacture soil from scratch, and all this while floating in the poisonous salt sea. These are the trees that fascinate Dillard, the ones that manage not only to survive, but to flourish amid conditions clearly opposed to their subsistence. Bit by bit, they gather to their bases pieces of muck that combine to form a sort of soil in which grow other trees and roots, and in which gather varieties of shells, fish, oysters, shrimp, birds and organic substances like guano. Soon the tree has become an island that:

wanders on, afloat and adrift. It walks teetering and wanton before the wind. Its fate and direction are random. It may bob across an ocean and catch on another mainland's shores. It may starve or dry while it is still a sapling. It may topple in a storm, or pitchpole. By the rarest of chances, it may stave into another mangrove island in a crash of clacking roots, and mesh. What it is most likely to do is drift anywhere in the alien ocean, feeding on death and growing, netting a makeshift soil as it goes, shrimp in its toes and terns in its hair. We could do worse. (150)

Not only could we do worse, in Dillard's view: the mangroves are metaphors for the human life lived against the backdrop of the vast and alien universe. Just as the mangroves manage to sometimes survive in the poisonous salt sea amid turbulent weather, so humans live in a natural environment that is often hostile to them. Dillard uses the phrase "we could do worse" as a transition to several paragraphs in which she pushes the similarity between mangrove islands and human lives. She begins:

I alternate between thinking of the planet as home—dear and familiar stone hearth and garden—and as a hard land of exile in which we are all sojourners. Today I favor the latter view . . . "For we are strangers before thee, and sojourners, as were all our fathers: our days on the earth are as a shadow, and there is none abiding." (150)

Here, she evokes again the passage from Psalms 39:12, the key passage for the sojourner motif that runs through much of Dillard's work. The earth is a "hard land of exile" to humans just as the ocean is "alien" and poisonous to the mangroves. She goes on:

We don't know where we belong, but in times of sorrow it doesn't seem to be here, here with these silly pansies and witless mountains, here with sponges and hard-eyed birds. In times of sorrow the innocence of the other creatures—from whom and with whom we evolved—seems a mockery. Their ways are not our ways. . . . It doesn't seem to be here that we belong, here where space is curved, the earth is round, we're all going to die, and it seems as wise to stay in bed as budge. It is strange here, not quite warm enough, or too warm, too leafy, or inedible, or windy, or dead. It is not, quite frankly, the sort of home for people one would have thought of—although I lack the fancy to imagine another. (151)

This passage explodes sentimental and romanticized visions of the earth as exclusively a place of growth, nurturance, and healing. Here, the earth is presented as a hostile and alien place in which humans are forced to live—if they live at all— a place not suited to human needs or comfort. Of course, for Dillard, to say such things about the earth is to, in effect, say them about God. When she says of pansies, sponges, birds, and mountains that "Their ways are not our ways," she is deliberately taking a phrase that one usually uses to describe God and applying it to what McFague calls "God's body": the planet and its creatures. Therefore, the earth and

God are experienced, often and simultaneously by humans everywhere, as inhospitable and malevolent, as "hostile and poisonous, as though it were impossible for our vulnerability to survive on these acrid stones" (152). Humans on the planet, like mangrove islands on the ocean, are blown about randomly by unseen forces that overpower and destroy human life in their wake. Even the planet itself is "a sojourner in airless space, a wet ball flung across nowhere" (151).

Dillard admits that these are "the thoughts of despair . . . [that] crowd back, unbidden, when human life as it unrolls goes ill, when we lose control of our lives or the illusion of control, and it seems that we are not moving toward any end but merely blown" (152). Bearing the despair in mind, Dillard manages to find "possibilities for beauty" (152) in such thoughts. Bearing in mind the poisonous salt sea and the harsh rocky world, she reifies the mangrove as a model for the human life lived in adverse conditions. Humans at their best should live like the mangrove: "exposed . . . beautiful and loose . . . turn[ing] drift into dance" (152). The image is not unlike that of the weasel being carried aloft to unknown places, his flesh dropping and his bones scattering. It is an image of abandonment to the given, daredevil adventure, and utter tenacity—all good characteristics to have when dealing with an earth and deity of the kind Dillard envisions.

Teaching a Stone to Talk, then, joins *Pilgrim at Tinker Creek* and *Holy the Firm* in presenting a model of deity that focuses not only on the analogies between the natural world and God, but on the harsh aspects of the natural world that are assumed to reveal God. The deadly and sovereign deity that Dillard imagines and/ or experiences in various encounters and epiphanic moments is one that she insists upon seeking regardless of the danger to herself or to conventional theology. For amidst the danger, in the path of the fiery blast, is the possibility for a transformation—mystical or otherwise—that does not negate or ignore the violence of the deity, but faces it squarely and even celebrates it. Readers get the chance to see this vision of a violent and deadly deity, and a human response to this deity, acted out in fictional form in Dillard's novel, *The Living*, which some critics erroneously regarded as thematically unrelated to her other work. As we shall see, not only are the theological themes in the novel completely in keeping with those of her other works, the novel presents those themes at their most vivid and disturbing.

Struggle, Death, and the Sojourner Motif

The Living is Dillard's ninth book and her first major work of fiction. It is set in the Bellingham Bay area of Washington state during the years 1855 to 1897. Her primary characters are a handful of families who were lured to this place of few mercies by its stunning beauty, its guarantee of adventure, and the possibility of untapped fortunes in farming and commerce. In the forty-year period on which Dillard focuses, settlers come and go, the coastal towns of Whatcom and Goshen boom and crash several times, and those brave souls who remain in the area try incessantly to carve out lives for themselves in a clearing they have somehow managed to wrest away from the thick fir trees whose trunks are the size of barns. The most significant thing, however, about these hearty people—called "the living"—is that they die. Moreover, God kills them; at least, this is the view of many of the settlers, most notably Ada Fishburn Tawes, who came to Whatcom from Illinois by wagon train in 1855 and never left. One could say that Ada is the theologian in the novel, for it is she who, in the first four pages of the book, expresses the theological understanding of the land to which they have come and its relation to God. In these first few pages, Dillard—via Ada—sets up the theological/scriptural themes that dominate the entire 400-page novel. These themes should be familiar to any reader of Dillard, for they form the deep theological premise of her other works discussed earlier.

Ada Fishburn steps off the schooner which had brought her and her family to Puget Sound. She stands silently while their possessions are off-loaded and stares at the ocean, the rough mountains, and the trees that come right to the shoreline. This, she thinks, is the "rough edge of the world" (3), a place that God created before he decided to make people, since clearly this was not a place intended to be inhabited by humans. Ada says to herself: "For we are strangers before thee, and sojourners, as were all our fathers; our days on earth are as a shadow, and there is none abiding" (4). This variation of Psalms 39:12 sets the scriptural tone for the entire novel, and introduces two significant aspects of Dillard's work. First, as in Dillard's other books discussed earlier, God is closely aligned with nature so that nature, in effect, becomes a model for God. In *The Living* as in *Holy the Firm*, God is modelled upon the landscape of Puget Sound; Ada Fishburn, therefore, when viewing her new home for the first time and citing Psalms 39:12, is addressing both God and nature. The "thee" of "we are strangers before thee" is both God and nature, or God as seen in nature.

Second, this passage sets up the sojourner motif that runs throughout the novel, a motif mentioned earlier in the chapter in connection with mangrove islands. A sojourner is a stranger or alien who stays only temporarily in a place. The word "sojourner," Dillard says, "invokes a nomadic people's sense of vagrancy, a praying people's knowledge of estrangement, a thinking people's intuition of sharp loss" (Dillard 1982b, 150).[5] Ada Fishburn is, at once, a nomadic, thinking and praying person who maintains her sense of herself—and everyone, for that matter—as a sojourner throughout her life in the novel. She, her husband and children, and other travelers coming to Puget Sound had "wandered in the desert like the Israelites . . . and prayed God would see them through" (Dillard 1982a, 191). The oxen vomited and died, men died at crossings or contracted chills or were trampled in buffalo stampedes, a young bride and her baby died of measles, and Ada's own son, Charley, was crushed under wagon wheels. On Sundays, they picked a preacher to read Scripture to them as they worked and "hoped God understood that they had to do these things straight through, so they could cross the mountains before it snowed" (192). Ada remembers:

Every single Sunday the preacher picked them out something to read about the Israelites' crossing the desert. God told them not to touch the mountain, in Sinai, or he would break forth against them. They did not touch the mountain, but it seemed like He broke forth against them anyway, as He broke forth against her in sight of the mountains, and she hadn't touched a thing, either. (192)

After settling in Puget Sound, her husband is killed by a natural gas leak while digging a well. Later, another of her children dies of an earache. Throughout the years, she and others observe how various members of the community are drowned in fishing vessels, crushed in logjams, burned to death, or otherwise killed in efforts to simply live in a land so lacking in mercies. The novel's narrator tells us of Ada's belief that "agricultural [work] hewed closer to God's plan for mankind than commerce ever could, though she could not say why, unless it was that the sight of people struggling without hope pleased Him, which would not surprise her" (100). Ada, then, very clearly sees herself and others as sojourners in a land not made with them in mind, and as strangers before a God who "press[es] down on them so hardly on earth" (129).

Later in the novel, Ada repeats to herself the sojourner passage from Psalms 39 as she reflects upon the overconfidence of new settlers who do not know, as she does, the list of casualties from her generation of settlers. They are too new to the place to know that "[t]he gravedigger's spade turn[s] up more earth than a plow" (189). She knows, as they do not, that she has "look[ed] up from wringing a chicken's neck . . . and [seen] God Almighty wringing a person's neck slowly, as if He had no sense, and didn't know the difference, and hadn't saved us people like He said, in his mercy" (189). She wearily meditates on the affirmation of Psalms 119, "It is good for me that I have been afflicted; that I might learn thy statutes" (191).

What statutes did she, Ada, need to learn that bad? Back in Illinois they had a neighbor who held his children's hands in the fire to impress lessons upon them. No one mistook that man for God, though he taught the same way. What statutes did Nettie need to learn, that her whimpering with the earache was good for her? Or Charley, [that he had to be killed under the wagon]? The statute about loving God? The statute about loving your neighbor? . . . It [is] too much to ask. (191)

At the end of her life, Ada remembers that her first husband used to have her read from the Scriptures: "I believe that I shall see the goodness of the Lord in the land of the living" (21). Now, years and dozens of deaths later, one might expect Ada to be bitter. On the contrary, she judges that she has lived a good life:

For she had truly felt God's power. Charley got killed in the rut. Nettie died . . . She buried two fine husbands. It was not everybody got so deep into the battering and jabbing of it all, got in the path of the great God's might. . . . She took part in the great drama. It had been her privilege to peer into the deepest well hole of life's surprise. She felt the fire of God's wild breath on her face (334).

Of course, the well hole here reminds us of the well in which her first husband died. Moreover, the image of God's fiery breath on her face makes of her a Moses-like figure who dares to go up into the mountain to see the back parts of God, and returns with his face burned and changed by God's presence. Such daring and "going into the gaps" is a topic Dillard gives considerable treatment in *Pilgrim at Tinker Creek*; one could even say it is the thesis of the book. The good life—the life most pure, honest, and worthy, the life Ada lived—is the life lived in full knowledge and experience of the death-wielding power of God via nature, and of the possibility of beauty and meaning that comes from that same source.

Ada is not the only character in the novel aware of the savage, merciless side of God and nature; all the settlers experience it, especially the early ones. Minta Honer, another of the early settlers and friend to Ada, sits on her porch one morning, shelling peas and basking in the beauty and peacefulness of the day; she calls it "a God-day" (106). That same day, the irony of this becomes apparent when her husband, Eustace, is killed in a logjam. Truly, it is a God-day. Weeks later, Minta reads passages from Isaiah to her children before putting them to bed: "'Have ye not known? Have ye not heard? . . . the inhabitants thereof are as grasshoppers . . . he shall also blow upon them, and they shall wither, and the whirlwind shall take them away as stubble'" (122). A few hours later, these same children are burned to death in her house. They, like Ada, felt the fire of God's wild breath and were blown away like grasshoppers. Months later, Minta learns about herself that when she kneels and gives prayers of thanksgiving to God, she is really expressing her fears more than any gratitude, because "[a]lthough she held that God gives blessings, she could recall no evidence—in Scripture, sermon, or history—that He preserves them, thanked or not" (140–1).

Clare Fishburn, Ada's son, becomes acutely aware of the ubiquity of death and reflects at great length on the fragility of life in the face of inevitable death. He, like his mother, finds himself quoting frequently from Isaiah after receiving a death threat from a lunatic intellectual type—Beal Obenchain—who lives on the outskirts of Whatcom. One might well argue that Beal Obenchain is a type for God in that he promises eventual death, and assumes God's voice in passages from the Hebrew prophets concerning the impending violence and destruction that God will soon deliver to the people. Clare lives in fear of death for several weeks, avoiding Obenchain, making plans for his soon-to-be abandoned family. Eventually, however, Clare realizes that he is going to die whether or not Obenchain kills him. Not only he, but everyone is going to die. Everyone is a terminal patient, and "[e]very place [is] a tilting edge" (197). As God has said through the prophet Isaiah: "'And I will wipe Jerusalem as a man wipeth a dish, wiping it and turning it upside down'" (197). Clare envisions God—or Obenchain, it really doesn't matter who— as a lion who will come and break his bones. When he reads of 36,000 people who die in a flood in Sumatra, Ada replies that they were all going to die anyway. At first, he is shocked, but later resigns himself to the eventuality of death and, further, death doled out by conditions of life on earth. His enlightenment is confirmed by an epiphany of sorts that he sees as he stands on the beach and looks back at fields being plowed. He watches two men walking behind plows, "turn[ing] the green ground under. Then . . . he saw the earth itself walking, the earth walking darkly as it always walks in every season: it was plowing the men under, and the horses, and the plows" (353). So, God, via the earth or nature, sustains humans for a short while, then plows them under with their possessions and begins a new crop. His old, dead mother—Ada—was right: "We are strangers before thee, and sojourners . . . our days on earth are as a shadow, and there is none abiding."

The sojourner motif is only one of a host of theological themes running through this novel and Dillard's work as a whole. Yet, it is the most important one, for it helps to underscore the savage, sinister, and arbitrary aspects of the deity she sees represented in nature. Clare Fishburn's response to this deity who deals in death is the appropriate one: he reorders his life toward acceptance of the frailty of all life, the givenness of death and cruelty, and, most importantly, toward the possibilities for meaning and freedom in this acceptance. Clare comes to the same conclusion at the end of *The Living* that Dillard herself reaches at the end of *Pilgrim*, when she finally understands that she is "dealing with a maniac" (270). This maniac, of course, is God exhibited in the cruel and exacting landscape of Puget Sound in *The Living*, the horrifying and beautiful exuberance of the created world in *Pilgrim*, and in the harsh cold and stillness of Antarctica in *Teaching*. "Divinity is not playful," Dillard concludes. If one accepts this fact—as Ada and Clare Fishburn do in the novel—one can be transformed, like the monk on the road mentioned in *Pilgrim*, "who knows precisely how vulnerable he is, who takes no comfort among death-forgetting men," and who will not part with his "vision of vastness" (270).

In conclusion, Dillard's models contrast sharply with those which reign in current political theological discourse, specifically the models typified by the work of McFague. While adhering to a scientific worldview that acknowledges the impartial and often brutal processes of evolution in the natural world, and while adamantly insisting upon aligning God or deity with the natural world that operates according to the law of evolution, among others, McFague still maintains a model of God that focuses upon love, healing, nurturance, and concern with human endeavor. I argue that such a position is inconsistent with its own premises; furthermore, it is in the work of Annie Dillard that we may find models of God more appropriate to a worldview that includes within it the aligning of deity and the natural world, and a contemporary scientific and evolutionary understanding of the cosmos.

A key feature of the Dillardian models of deity that is lost in McFague's models is the feature of otherness. Dillard's models of God, while affirming the immanence of deity in nature, nevertheless retain a sense of otherness in reference to God and to nature so that both are at times experienced as hostile or alien to humanity. When the world in which we live and the deity that is immanent in it seem hostile and alien, there is no room for fancying that the world or God is aligned in the least with human political or social concern. The otherness of God and the natural world appears most alarmingly in these instances, and serves as a critique of those models of God that are reductionistic and self-serving, focusing as they do only upon the aspects of deity that are comforting and helpful. While Dillard's models of deity retain a notion of otherness, one finds an explication of otherness much more thorough than Dillard's in the work of Emmanuel Levinas. Mapping his philosophical categories onto the Dillardian meditation on nature throws otherness in nature and deity into sharper relief, and exposes the utilitarian aspects of many political, specifically liberationist, models of deity. Such is the task of the next chapter.

Notes

1. It should be explained that throughout her works, Dillard often mentions attending church services. Some of the services are Catholic, some are Episcopalian, others are Congregationalist. Whatever service she is attending at the time of her writing is the one most likely to show up in her work.

2. These are themes that cast an interesting spin on Levinas's notion of the elemental, which I will focus upon in a later chapter.

3. This second story is titled "The Venture of Prayer" and is found in Martin Buber's *Tales of the Hasidim:The Early Masters* (New York: Schocken Books, 1947): 275–6. Dillard is quite fond of these stories of the Hasidim, so fond that she repeats them in her book *The Writing Life* (New York: Harper and Row, 1988).

4. Passivity, in the weasel passage, is complicated by the weasel's act of seizing. Dillardian spirituality, likewise, is a complicated passivity in that it involves not only submitting to the blasts of deity, but actively stalking the deity tenaciously and skillfully.

5. The sojourner motif resonates with the nomadic sensibility in much postmodernist thinking, for example, Derrida's comments in "Plato's Pharmacy" on the waywardness of the son who, having left the father, "can no longer repeat his origin" (Derrida 1981, 144). Specifically, the sojourner motif in Dillard resembles the nomadic wandering of Abraham as he is described by Levinas, as one who goes out from his home to an alien land and never even allows his servants to return. Abraham's nomadism is indicative of his openness to the Other and disregard for the utility of his journey. See Levinas 1986, 346–9.

Chapter 4

God and the Elemental in Levinas

> O how powerful is the pure love of Jesus, which is mixed with no self-interest, nor self-love! Are not all those to be called mercenary, who are ever seeking consolations? Do they not show themselves to be rather lovers of themselves than of Christ, who are always thinking of their own profit and advantage? Where shall one be found who is willing to serve God for nought?
> —Thomas á Kempis, *Of The Imitation of Christ*

Emmanuel Levinas, shaped by the phenomenological tradition of Husserl and Heidegger's account of Being, is known primarily for his articulation of radical alterity and its role within an ethical metaphysics. Levinas's conception of the Other, another person as bearer of radical alterity, has helped shape recent French thought and is enjoying fresh interest on the part of American thinkers. Levinas's concept of the *elemental*, however, is not as well known as his notion of the radically Other. In this chapter, I first want to explore the relation between the elemental, as Levinas conceives of it, and the radical alterity of the Other. I will discuss Levinas's concept of the elemental, paying special attention to his articulation of it in terms of what he calls faceless pagan gods and his refusal to attribute radical alterity to it. I argue that despite Levinas's refusal, the elemental does conceal a strain of radical alterity and can thus be seen as an Other and, paradoxically, as the location of the transcendent divine. Identifying the natural world as a possible Other in Levinas's thought allows for a mapping of the Levinasian categories of otherness and violence onto the Dillardian corpus in a way that highlights, first, the otherness of nature and deity in Dillard's work as well as the violence perpetrated by that nature/deity and, second, the reductive aspects of much recent theologizing when deity is conceived of from within the context of the cosmos.

The Elemental and Otherness

The term 'elemental' in Levinas refers to earth, air, sea, and light.[1] It is the world from which we conduct our business, specifically the business of representation, possession and the building of the domicile. The elemental is the medium from which things of possession or representation come to us, and this medium is "a common fund or terrain, essentially non-possessable" (Levinas 1969, 131). One can gain a foothold in the elemental by, for example, cultivating a field, navigating the sea, or fishing from the river, but these activities do not utterly reduce the elemental to a thing. The elemental remains essentially non-possessable even as the 'sides' of it, such as the "the surface of the sea and of the field, the edge of the wind" (131), are used for certain ends. Every use, relation or possession of these 'sides' of the elemental is situated within the larger milieu which cannot be contained, belongs to nobody, and envelops all other relations and containments. The elemental "envelops or contains without being able to be contained or enveloped" (131).

Enjoyment, for Levinas, is life lived within the elemental, bathed in the non-possessable milieu "from which they [things of representation] emerge and to which they return in the enjoyment we can have of them" (130). In enjoyment, one leaves the safety of the domicile and plunges into the elemental without regard for future ends. Enjoyment is "an ultimate relation with the substantial plenitude of being, with its materiality" (133), and activity in this mode "does not derive its meaning and its value from an ultimate and unique goal" (133). Life in the elemental—life in enjoyment—is life lived "without utility, in pure loss, gratuitously, without referring to anything else, in pure expenditure—this is the purely human" (133). Furthermore, life in enjoyment is characterized by a "carefreeness with regard to existence" (134) and by a deafness to the Other. In enjoyment, the Ego is only for itself, innocently and with abandon. The Ego is outside all communication with the Other, "without ears, like a hungry stomach" (134).

The above reference to the Other—capital 'O'—draws our attention not only to the Ego's lack of communication with the Other in the state of enjoyment, but also, and more importantly for this discussion, to the language Levinas uses when speaking of the elemental and its resistance to being possessed. His description of the elemental in this regard resembles his articulation of the radical alterity of the Other. Before furthering this line of thinking, let us review Levinas's conception of the Other and radical alterity.

Levinas's goal is the redefining of metaphysics in terms of ethics. His version of metaphysics, rescued from the reductions of ontology and phenomenology, begins when it criticizes itself as a totalizing ontology or a philosophy of power. Traditional phenomenology and ontology are economies of the same, according to Levinas, and are afflicted with desires to see, to know, to have, and to will. These are words of violence for Levinas; they are also words of plenitude and presence, what Derrida would call expressions of logocentrism (Cohen 1986, 20). Levinas says western philosophy has always been struck with the horror of the Other—"an insurmountable allergy"—so that the Other is manifested as a being and thus loses its alterity. Heideggerian thought, specifically, sees comprehension of Being as the aim of existence, and the Other here appears as a being among other beings. The Other in Heidegger's scenario swims in the pool of Being and the I is like Ulysses who, through all his adventures, returns home to himself, is only on the way to his native island. Abraham, on the other hand, leaves his homeland forever for a yet unknown land and forbids his servant even to bring back his son to the point of departure. This (Abraham's) is a movement without return, a movement of the same or the I to the Other which never returns to the same, a one-way movement; this is to act without entering into the promised land (Levinas 1986, 346–9). It is a movement of expenditure, of loss, which resonates with the language Levinas uses to describe the life of enjoyment in the elemental, a life lived gratuitously, in pure loss, without regard for future utility.[2]

In refusing Heidegger's Being of beings as the home of the Other, Levinas speaks of the Other as being beyond Being, a third 'person'[3] who escapes the bipolar play of immanence and transcendence, revealing and concealing, etc., that is common to Heideggerian ontological thinking (Levinas 1986, 356). The Other comes from beyond the horizon of Being, from beyond the world and involves a signification of its own, independent from that of the world (Derrida 1978, 103). The Other not only visits us outside of a received context, but comes without mediation: the Other signifies itself. The Other is infinity, an overflowing of ontology, a breaking of the bounds of ontology, an irreducibleness of infinity even to the concept of infinity (98). Levinas explains the homologous nature of the relation between alterity and infinity in "Philosophy and the Idea of the Infinite," an essay I will return to later in this section. Here, Levinas explains that when one thinks of infinity, one thinks of *more* than one thinks, because infinity exceeds the word or idea 'infinity'. He says, "Infinity does not enter into the *idea* of infinity, is not grasped; this idea is not a concept. The infinite is the radically, absolutely, other" (54). The otherness of infinity, then, is demonstrated in that it exceeds any attempts, linguistically or cognitively, to grasp it.[4]

The subjectivity for the I that is generated in Levinas's ethical metaphysics is, naturally, an ethical rather than an ontological subjectivity. In ontological subjectivity, the I, the self, exists as a monad, stabilized in its own intelligibility and its own consciousness of itself and of other beings like itself. Ethical subjectivity, on the other hand, sees the I as being from the beginning called into question by the Other, having already done violence to the Other in acts of cognition and representation. The face of the Other puts the consciousness of the I into question. The I loses its sovereignty, its single identification, in which the I goes out from itself and returns to itself triumphantly to rest. To be an I in ethical subjectivity means not being able to slip away from responsibility to the Other, not being able to block out the plea of the Other to spare its life (Levinas 1986, 353).

According to Derrida, the Other in Levinas signals "the emergence of absolute, radical alterity, the emergence of an exteriority that can be neither derived, nor engendered, nor constituted on the basis of anything other than itself" (Derrida 1978, 106). Hence, Levinas's work is a dismantling and a dispossession of a system of totality under which the Other is subsumed and domesticated (82). The Other, in Levinas'ss ethical metaphysics, is not possessed, enslaved, and made to serve the ends of utility, and in this respect the Other resembles the elemental. Remember that even when a side of the elemental, such as the wave of the sea or the edge of the wind, is put to use or is understood according to its laws of operation, the elemental is still not thereby possessed or utterly tamed. It remains in its unknowable depth, its resistance to being owned, and its refusal to be circumnavigated. Neither the Other nor the elemental are to be domesticated.

Another level of similarity exists between the Other and the elemental in Levinas, however, that has to do not with the activity of the I in regard to either of them, but with the respective 'effects', for lack of a better term, that the Other and the elemental have upon the I. Concerning the Other, Levinas is adamant about exposing the violence that the I of ontological subjectivity does to the Other in acts of cognition and representation, by reducing the Other to a content of consciousness. In addition to this level of violence, however, there exists another level of violence that is allowable: the violence the Other does to the I's domesticating and reductive concepts and formulations. The Other exposes the I in an epiphanic visitation and utterly destroys the philosophical framework in which the I had tried to enframe it. On this level, violence is not being done to the Other, but by the Other, and it is a violence that ends in illuminating the radical alterity of the Other and its refusal to be domesticated.

In a similar way, the elemental becomes an agent of violence and death as easily as it becomes one of enjoyment. The elemental becomes menacing when the very aspects of it that give rise to enjoyment and gratuitous expenditure change and begin to deal in violence. As Edith Wyschogrod explains, "the same force which sustains pleasure turns with alarming suddenness into a power of death and destruction. The destructive potential of sea, sky, wind threatens the very existence which seeks to enjoy them" (Wyschogrod 1973, 168). The tools with which one tries to "gain a foothold" in the elemental, such as the plow, boat, or plane, are exposed as being puny and trivial, a mere scratch on the surface of the depth that is the elemental. The elemental holds both enjoyment and death in its power, and cannot be roped into withholding death in order to alleviate the insecurity of the Ego. As the Other exposes to the I the limits and violence of the latter's acts of cognition, so the elemental, by being what it is, exposes the limits of the Ego's enjoyment. At the core of both exposures is the Other's and the elemental's resistance to domestication and insistence on remaining ultimate strangers to the I and Ego.

In fact, as Levinas states, it is when one "runs up against the very strangeness of the earth" (Levinas 1969, 142) that one realizes the limit of enjoyment, experiences insecurity, and is prompted to separate from the primordial bathing in the elemental and establish the domicile. It is at this moment of recognizing the strangeness of the elemental that what lurks behind the 'side' of the elemental is revealed. Levinas claims that "what the side of the element that is turned toward me conceals is not a 'something' susceptible of being revealed, but an ever-new depth of absence, an existence without existent, the impersonal par excellence" (142). The elemental extends into a nothingness, a "nocturnal prolongation" (142), into what Levinas calls the *il y a*, or the 'there is'. The nothingness that is the 'there is,' and the insecurity derived from the experience of it, are expressed in the faceless, mythical, pagan gods of the elemental; these gods mark the limits of enjoyment. The gods in the elemental, thus extended to the 'there is', are faceless because of the lack of existent in this kind of existence, an absence that is a presence of a sort (Levinas 1978, 58). The utter impersonality of the 'there is', and the fact that the elemental is "indifferent to the gratification which it provides" (Wyschogrod 1974, 168) cause Levinas to conceive of the gods of the elemental as faceless, unapproachable, and gods "to whom one does not speak" (Levinas 1969, 142). Since these gods of the elemental and the 'there is' are without a face and impersonal, they lack a fundamental quality for *homo religiosus*, that is, transcendence. As Wyschogrod explains, "it is the need for transcendence which characterizes fully human ethical existence . . . and it is founded in the experience of other persons [or the Other]" (Wyschogrod 1974, 57, insertion mine). Therefore, while the elemental and its extension, the 'there is', have a definite otherness and strangeness, their otherness is not, in Levinas's view, the radical alterity of the Other. The distinction between the otherness of the elemental and the radical alterity of the Other centers around the fact that the latter has a face and, thus, provides the possibility of transcendence for the ethical subject in one-way relation. The gods of the elemental, having no faces, do not exhibit such a radical alterity. Here, then, the resemblance between the elemental and the Other ends, at least in Levinas's view.

The otherness that Levinas does, in fact, attribute to the elemental is a lower case variety. The menacing aspects of the elemental "disturb it [the Ego] as the *other*, and . . . it [the Ego] will appropriate [this otherness] by recollecting in a dwelling" (Levinas 1969, 137, Levinas'semphasis). In other words, the I is shaken by encountering the dangerous aspects of the elemental and tries, then, to minimized the danger by creating a safe place for itself. Levinas goes on to say that "enjoyment seems to be in touch with an 'other' inasmuch as a future is announced within the element and menaces it with insecurity" (137). As explained above, Levinas distinguishes the otherness of the elemental from the radical alterity of the Other, mainly because of its facelessness. I want to argue, however, that the elemental does have a face of a sort, and that in Levinas's own writings he conflates the otherness of the elemental or nature with radical alterity.

Such a conflation can be seen most clearly in his essay "Philosophy and the Idea of the Infinite." In this essay, Levinas articulates his understanding of western philosophy as narcissistic in that it grants 'primacy to the same'. By this Levinas means that this type of philosophy, which sees itself as a philosophy of freedom, "presupposes that freedom itself is sure of its right, is justified without recourse to anything further, is complacent in itself, like Narcissus" (49). When narcissistic philosophy comes upon something other than itself, when "there arises a term foreign to the philosophical life . . . it becomes an obstacle . . . [and] has to be integrated into this life" (49). Here, again, is another articulation of the western philosophical monad reducing the radical alterity of the Other to familiar terms, except in this particular text, to make a surface observation, Levinas uses the lower case 'o' to talk about the foreign term—which is clearly the *O*ther—that confronts narcissistic philosophy. Furthermore, and more importantly, Levinas connects this other to forces in the elemental. He describes the other, the foreign term later reduced to the same by philosophy, as: "the land that supports us and disappoints our efforts, the sky that elevates us and ignores us, the forces of nature that aid us and kill us, things that encumber us or serve us, men who love us and enslave us" (49). Three of the five examples—and this is *the Other* about which he is speaking—exemplify alterity in terms of nature and the forces of the elemental. The forces of the elemental, which, as explained earlier, have both the capacity to aid and to kill—these faceless, impersonal forces—are here used as examples of the alterity that a philosophy of the same wishes to reduce in order to alleviate the threat to the freedom of the cognitive monad. Thanks to the reductive activity of narcissism, "these realities [the other, the forces of the elemental], whose plaything I am in danger of becoming, are understood [cognized and reduced] by me" (49).

In this particular text, then, the radical alterity of that which opposes western narcissistic philosophy, and the otherness of the forces of the elemental, are conflated and not distinguished from each other. This can be argued in spite of the assertion Levinas makes earlier in the essay, when speaking generally about the desire for and movement toward "the stranger" which is the Other, that one moves "beyond the nature that surrounds us . . . [which] in complicity with men, submits to their reasons and inventions; in it men also feel themselves to be at home" (47). Indeed, a distinguishing trait of Levinas's thought is that "against the Heideggerian philosophy of a primordial anxiety . . . Levinas posits a self at home with itself, satiable and happy" (Wyschogrod 1974, 56). The world, including nature, that surrounds us often feels safe and is the source of enjoyment, as earlier explained. Levinas's own articulation of the elemental, however, includes the eventual dissolution of sheer enjoyment when the ego comes up against menacing forces contained within the very world it deems safe. The elemental, in short, becomes the stranger. Thus, Levinas's conception of the world and the elemental as safe and familiar, while serving his philosophical agenda and distinguishing him from Heidegger, turns itself on its own head later when Levinas describes the change in the elemental from the familiar and safe to the strange and threatening.

Let us return to Levinas's essay, "Philosophy and the Idea of Infinity." He goes on to identify "a second characteristic of the philosophy of the same: its recourse to neuters" (50). The neuter allows the I to gain access to the non-I, the foreign or other, through an entity or "abstract essence which is and is not," and in which "is dissolved the other's alterity" (50). With the aid of the neuter—the abstract essence—the I cognizes in the other something allegedly familiar or recognizable by which to capture the other. In such cognizing, the alterity of the other fades and the foreign becomes the familiar. Once again, Levinas gives examples of the other that is reduced in violent acts of cognition demonstrated by the use of the neuter. "To know [to cognize in a reductive way]" he states, "is to surprise in the individual confronted, in this wounding stone, this upward plunging pine, this roaring lion, that by which it is not this very individual, this foreigner" (50). To know is to (allegedly) see in the other something (the neuter) that indicates that it is not, in fact, a foreigner. Levinas gives four examples of the foreigner, three of which are derived from nature and thus bound up with the elemental: the stone that wounds, the growing pine, and the roaring lion. Once again, Levinas uses images from the elemental to express his ideas about radical alterity, thereby eliminating, it would seem, the rigid distinction between the radical alterity of the Other and the otherness of the elemental. Examples taken from nature—from the elemental—serve Levinas in his articulation of the violence done to radical alterity in acts of cognition and representation.

Still left to consider, however, is the issue of the facelessness of the elemental, and the limit to transcendence that Levinas claims is put in place by this facelessness. As earlier explained, Levinas sees the nothingness of the 'there is' expressed in mythical, impersonal, and allegedly primitive gods who are faceless. The elemental, as Levinas explains, does not have a face, but a 'side'. The translator's note explains that the French word translated 'side' is actually *visage*, the word for 'face' that Levinas usually uses in reference to the countenance of the Other. Levinas, via translation, says of the elemental: "it is content without form. Or rather it has but a side: the surface of the sea and of the field, the edge of the wind; the medium upon which this side** takes form is not composed of things" (131). The translator clearly sought to make a distinction between the face of the Other and the face of the elemental, "to reserve the English word 'face' to translate *visage*—the countenance of the Other" (131). The fact, however, that *visage* is the word Levinas uses for both the Other and the elemental indicates that the elemental may not be as faceless as he claims.

A reference to the face occurs again in "Philosophy and the Idea of Infinity," the same essay in which Levinas uses examples from nature to illustrate radical alterity. Here, when speaking of the recourse to neuters, he explains that the neuter allows a philosophy of the same to know the Other, so that "the foreign being, instead of maintaining itself in the inexpugnable fortress of its singularity, instead of *facing*, becomes a theme and an object" (50, emphasis mine). Levinas, then, moves one sentence later to give the four examples, previously noted, of the foreign that is not allowed to 'face', three of which are drawn from nature or the elemental. Again, then, Levinas attributes some degree of 'faceness' to the elemental despite his assertion that the gods of the elemental are faceless.[5]

Finally, the distinction Levinas makes between the radical alterity of the Other, which contains within it the possibility of transcendence, and the (alleged) facelessness and lower case otherness of the elemental is called into question by an argument Derrida makes in reference to Levinas's use of the term 'infinite' for the Other. Robert Bernasconi explains that "Levinas attempts to think the Other not by negation but as a positive plenitude; and yet, as Derrida observes, he is nevertheless obliged to use the negative word—'infinity'—to do it" (Bernasconi 1988, 15). Furthermore, according to Derrida, the word 'infinite' contains within it the term 'finite', indicating that the two terms cannot be utterly opposed to each other, but must be seen as defined in reference to one another. Levinas, then, cannot say that the Other is infinitely and absolutely other; the most he can say is that the Other "must be other than myself" (Derrida 1978, 126). If, in Levinas's thought, 'infinite' stands for the radically Other, and 'finite' stands for a totalizing philosophy of the same, Derrida's critique of such a binary demonstrates how "the infinite [is drawn] back into the sphere of philosophy," or how the utter opposition between the infinite Other and a finite totalizing philosophy cannot be rigidly maintained (Bernasconi 1988, 15). I suggest that just as the infinite/finite binary is drawn into relational reciprocity and thus does not stand, neither does the opposition between the transcendent and the elemental, or the 'face-full' and the faceless. Just as the infinite is marked by the finite, so is the transcendent marked by the elemental, so that they are not utterly opposed and distinguished from each other. In fact, they bear the mark of each other. The impersonal gods of the elemental bear the marks of transcendence in that there emerges here and there among them a 'side' of a countenance—even a trace of a face—that shocks and destabilizes, and calls the Ego or I into question.[6]

I suggest that the elemental and the Other in Levinas share in radical alterity, despite his assertions to the contrary. While Levinas allows for what I have called a lower case otherness in the elemental, I have tried to show that the otherness of the elemental actually resembles the radical alterity of the Other, and that the division between the elemental and the transcendent cannot be so simply drawn. In short, in my reading of Levinas, nature can be posited as an Other; furthermore, when this idea is mapped across the terrain of Dillard's work, in which a radically other deity is revealed in the natural world, such Dillardian assertions gain extra edge and sharpness. Levinas's explication of the Other and the violence in relation to the Other reveals a deity who is radically other than human beings, ultimately refuses to be domesticated, and is revealed, despite Levinas's disclaimers, as such most profoundly in the elemental or the natural world. In addition, those who would represent deity in a reductive fashion that serves primarily certain political and social objectives are exposed in their violent acts of utility and possession. The deity that is revealed or metaphorized by the elemental Other—the natural world— cannot ultimately be conceived of in terms of human desires and goals any more than the plowed field or the navigated river can be said to ultimately serve the purposes of those who use it for their own ends. Deity, the field, the river—all exceed the acts of utility that seek to tame them.[7]

The Theology of Defamiliarization

Peter Fritzell, in his book *Nature Writing in America: Essays upon a Cultural Type*, speaks of Dillard's project in *Pilgrim* in terms that often resonate with issues raised about strangeness and familiarity, the other and the same, and so on in Levinas's work. He says of Dillard:

> No figure in American nature writing is more openly (if not obsessively) engaged in resisting such sanctioned forms of settlement, none more given (or driven) to unsettling things and to keeping them unsettled. . . . None is more resistant to the processes and methods of conventional explanation, or more disposed to the wild and extreme, to the manifestly unexplainable. . . . and especially, perhaps, to the indisputably predatory and bloodied, the bitten and bloated, the flighty, the frenzied, and even on occasion the feral. . . . no figure in American nature writing is more patently off her rocker—nor, in deeply traditional ways, more often on it. (218–9)

Fritzell goes on:

> Certainly no work commonly aligned with nature writing [*Pilgrim*] does more to prove that the attempt to settle oneself in America—the effort to compose oneself and to fix the terms of one's environment, in this country so especially dedicated to human individuality and nonhuman other—is finally an epistemological and metaphysical struggle, an ongoing psychobiotic and philosophic scramble in which virtually every moment of innerving belief and hope is met with a coordinate moment of unnerving doubt, each instance of stabilizing facticity . . . followed by a meditation on the fragility and indeterminacy of fact, each image of energizing beauty or harmony accompanied by reminders of wasteful and wasting profligacy. (219)

To summarize, Dillard's project is to show that the familiar is actually strange, that what seems sometimes to be in accordance with human hope is actually other and alien, and that one is most deeply within the arms of narcissistic denial when one fancies that the natural environment in which we live is suited ultimately and without qualification to human endeavor and determination. Furthermore, and more importantly, the deity that is revealed by the often alien natural world, likewise, is not calibrated to human desire and fulfillment, but rather often seems hostile to them. In this realization, the confidence of those who conceive of deity in terms only of love, mercy, and nurturance is destabilized; the realization of a hostile, or even indifferent, world and deity does violence to any notion of sweet ideological communion between the human and the divine. In such realization, we become aware acutely of "a cosmos and a wilderness forever opposed to our settling down or in" (221); we realize that what we thought was *"terra firma"* is actually *"terra incognita"* (221).[8]

Fritzell notes the story Dillard tells about the first day of her French class, when she was a child, and she "fondly imagined that all foreign languages were codes for English," but then realized after the first day that she was "going to have to learn speech all over again. . . . to start all over again, on a new continent, learning the strange syllables one by one" (228, qtd. Dillard 1974, 104–7). She learned that French words may never totally make sense in English, but only in their own language; they may be ultimately untranslatable. Of course Dillard stretches this observation to the natural world—in this case, springtime—and asserts that springtime may not be totally decipherable in our received understandings and languages, that we may have to try to learn, or at least get a glimpse of, another way to see and think about springtime. She then proceeds to try her hand at that 'other' understanding. The point here is that at this moment in *Pilgrim* there is yet another indicator of the otherness of the natural world—even in something as seemingly benign as springtime—which, by extension, indicates the otherness of deity. Importantly, the limits of language in reference to both nature and deity are exposed, as well as the tendency toward comfort and convention when speaking about an 'other'.

Fritzell summarizes well when he states that Dillard's work reflects

> a more or less constant struggle—on the one hand, to establish and maintain a sense of self and a capacity for self-consciousness, and independence and a feisty originality that cannot be explained or explained away—on the other hand, to establish and maintain the independent, unconditional existence of the other, *as a set of phenomena in no sense tied to (or dependent upon) one's own motivations or compositions*—and all the while sustaining one's belief in the prospect of utterly losing one's self (and one's sense of self) in the other. (231, emphasis mine)

The Dillardian self that drives itself to "really see" the world and experience it to the fullest; the alien and sometimes hostile other that is the natural world and the deity revealed in it; and the passive self that, like Simone Weil's good student, fixes itself in concentration so fastly that it loses itself entirely in a studious devotion, or is taken up like Dillard's weasel—these are the three main components in Dillard's account, all maintained simultaneously. The component that I see missing from political theology done in the liberationist vein of McFague's is the second component—the radically other natural world and deity—and this despite the fact that, for McFague, deity is revealed in the natural world. The natural world and the deity revealed in it simply do not retain an adequate measure of otherness in McFague's thought, and the thought of those who work within the parameters she has masterfully laid out in *Models of God*, *The Body of God*, and *Super/Natural Christians*. Weeding out otherness assures that all notions of violence, savagery, and destruction in reference to deity are excised from the models for God because they offend the current political and social comfort zone. These features of a model of God are banished despite the blatant evidence to the contrary. To accomplish what McFague claims she wants to accomplish in *The Body of God*—"to take the cosmos as the context for doing theology" (40)—means taking *all* of its aspects into account, the familiar and the strange, the benevolent and the hostile or indifferent, the comforting and the distressful. God the Ravager cannot be exiled any more than can God the Lover; Dillard's God of brute force, God as "one G" cannot be locked away so that God the Mother and Friend can live in peace. These discomforting 'other' gods must be maintained alongside the healing and nurturing ones in order to attempt truly to "take the cosmos as the context for doing theology" and to talk honestly about deity. To do otherwise is to do violence to otherness, to reduce the wildness and cruelty of the natural world—and the deity modeled upon it—to what in Levinasian terms might be called a representation of the same, and to take what ultimately is not tied to human endeavor and use it exclusively as an object of utility in a political, social *telos*.[9]

Levinas's account of the elemental as the context of enjoyment that can suddenly turn into an agent of death and destruction conforms, in important respects, with the view of nature championed by Dillard. Both Levinas's elemental and Dillard's nature are "indifferent to the gratification which [they] provide" (Wyschogrod 1973, 168). Conversely, they must be indifferent, as well, to the suffering they cause, both human and otherwise. Such a statement offends, perhaps, only momentarily when one thinks only of a falling tree, or crushing avalanche. Such events in nature are not usually, in the Western mindset, ascribed any kind of agency or intentionality. Whenever nature, and the events contained within it, are deemed as indicative of deity, however, tragic events such as earthquakes, cyclones, and avalanches take on a sharper, more offensive edge. Such random and indiscriminatory events in nature expose the limits of a model of deity rooted in benevolence and highlight the utter indifference to human comfort and happiness of the power manifested in the natural world, or the elemental. Events such as these, as Levinas asserts, demonstrate vividly a natural world of forces "whose plaything I am in danger of becoming" (Levinas 1987b, 49). Indeed, in both Dillard's and Levinas's conception of the natural world—although, Dillard's more than Levinas's—human beings and their concerns, however just, are treated with no more respect than the lives and concerns of certain insects or animals. Truly, the universe is not anthropocentric, but theocentric, if one takes the natural world as indicative of deity. Nature (and deity) serve themselves more than they serve the individual; in fact, sometimes it seems that any advantage or aid humans receive or wrest away from nature comes only accidentally and under nature's protest. As Dillard claims in *Holy the Firm* and fictively demonstrates in *The Living*, in times of tragedy, when loved ones have been maimed and killed, and we ourselves are broken by the forces of nature—by what she calls "conditions"—the world in which we live seems less like home and more like a land of hard, exacting exile.

Only a theology or philosophy primarily mindful of its own concerns would assert that deity is revealed most clearly in the natural world, and then attribute to that deity only traits of benevolence and goodness. As explained above, Levinas defines narcissistic philosophy as a philosophy that reduces radical alterity—revealed in a myriad of ways including the human face and forces of nature—to a term or entity of the same, or of the familiar. Narcissistic philosophy, when confronted with the foreigner, integrates the foreign into the familiar so that the foreign no longer stands as an obstacle to the objectives of the philosophizing monad. Can it not be said that a theology which excises those attributes of the natural world and of deity it finds objectionable is, in fact, narcissistic? Can it not be argued that a theology that privileges its own social and political goals over against the features of otherness disclosed by the elemental and the deity modeled upon it, features utterly indifferent or even hostile to any human political and social goals—can it not be said that such a theology differs scarcely from the reductive philosophy of the same of which Levinas speaks?

Clearly, I argue here for strong and definite parallels between various American political theologies, specifically liberationist theologies, and narcissistic philosophy as Levinas conceives of it. In arguing for such parallels, I am not unmindful, one, of the violence I do to Levinas's work even as I appropriate it to expose the violence of another. Indeed, every reading is an appropriation, mine no less than any other. Secondly, I do not intend to say that one can simply lay Levinas's work over that of Dillard's—as if it were a template designed especially for that purpose—and ignore the aspects of his work that are incommensurate with a Dillardian worldview. The most obvious instance of this I have already exposed: the fact that I use Levinas to speak of the radical alterity of nature, or the elemental, when he claims he reserves such a feature for a human Other. To read Dillard in the spirit of Levinas seems important, however, because of the way in which doing so illumines an ethical aspect of theologizing that is often ignored. Recent political theologizing, including many American feminist versions, aptly shows how certain theological motifs in western religion are actualized in unethical and unjust ways in society, especially for marginalized groups. These are important observations and criticisms that I do not mean to negate here. What is overlooked, however, are the ways in which the theologizing meant to correct these unethical and unjust tendencies actually results in *another* injustice in that it violently reduces and dismembers the ground of its own theologizing, namely nature and the deity that is modelled upon it. It is this ethical dimension that my mapping of Levinas onto Dillard is meant to illumine. To be ethical for Levinas and to be pure for Dillard both involve the same thing: being open to the Other.

Alterity, Nature, and Deconstruction

Openness to the Other or to radical alterity is, perhaps surprisingly for some, one way in which Derrida conceives of his project of deconstruction. Thinking of deconstruction in this way helps to underscore certain affinities or commensurabilities between Dillard's religious vision and the impulse of deconstruction, affinities which become clearer later. Such an underscoring requires careful qualification, for the disparities in thought between Dillard and Derrida are legion. Chief among these disparities is the fact that the Platonic and Neoplatonic tradition, with which Dillard aligns herself, is the prime example of the ontotheological tradition against which Derrida aims his critique of presence. The ways in which Derrida's critique would cut into the various epiphanic and pleromatic experiences Dillard narrates in *Pilgrim* and elsewhere are not difficult to imagine. Furthermore, to the extent that Dillard evokes the *via negativa*, the philosophical differences between her work and his hinge on the difference between deconstruction and negative theology, a difference strongly upheld but nevertheless debated.[10] Of course the most obvious disparity between the two lies in their subject matter. Dillard's subject is the natural world as a source of beauty and religious meaning; Derrida's is the history of Western philosophy and its various totalizations. Therefore, when I say that there are certain affinities between Dillard and Derrida, I am not unaware of the vast discrepancies in their thought. Nor do I wish to claim an easy affinity between them that glosses over the finer distinctions in their work respectively. What I mean to claim is this: One of the many ways in which Derrida explains his project of deconstruction, which I will show shortly, is in terms of an ethic of openness to the Other. When thought of in this way, it is possible to see some similarity between the impulse of deconstruction and that of Dillard's project as I have described it in this work so far. In no way do I argue that Dillard's theology is a purely postmodern one, although one might claim with some legitimacy, as I will do momentarily, that her religious vision approaches the postmodern in certain specific ways. I argue only that Derridean deconstruction and Dillardian religion, when seen in the light of a Levinasian ethic of openness to the Other, share an *impulse* that they manifest and work out in different sites and with dissimilar methods. This impulse is my concern here.

Deconstruction can be "defined" variously depending upon the particular discipline in which the deconstructive technique is operative. For example, deconstruction may appear as a variety of post-structuralism in literary studies, or as a critique of the metaphysics of presence and the ontotheological tradition built upon it in a philosophy or religious studies department, or as an antipode to functional structures in an architecture firm. Even specifically Derridean deconstruction, rather than relying upon a master trope to represent it, opts for a chain of signifiers, i.e., hymen, cinder, pharmakon, etc., to evoke not a system to replace those it criticizes, but a technique, sensibility, or critique applied to such systems. Despite the difficulty in saying what deconstruction *is*, one can safely argue that Derridean deconstruction concerns itself with what Derrida calls *differance*. *Differance* as well can be explained in a myriad of ways; for my purposes here, however, perhaps it is best to explain it as that which exposes the limits of identity as it is defined in western philosophy. Here, perhaps more than anywhere,

Derrida's indebtedness to Levinas begins to show, for it is western metaphysics' construction of identity that has provoked Levinas into proposing ethics rather than ontology as first philosophy. *Differance* exposes the ways in which identity is constructed at the expense of things that would threaten its unity and wholeness. *Differance* deconstructs traditional western identity construction—rooted in the self-contained, fully self-conscious ego—and shows it to have suppressed and excluded that which would hinder its development, namely, the Other. Therefore, in Richard Kearney's words, deconstruction in this context "contrives to dismantle our preconceived notions of *identity* and expose us to the challenge of hitherto suppressed or concealed 'otherness'—the *other* side of experience, which has been ignored in order to preserve the illusion of truth as a perfectly self-contained and self-sufficient presence" (Kearney 1986, 106). In his dialogue with Kearney, Derrida explains deconstruction in terms of this openness to the Other and, in doing so, shows his complicity with a Levinasian ethic.

Early in the dialogue, Derrida notes that his primary interest in Levinas's work lies in "posing the question of the 'other' to phenomenology" (108). In this vein, he goes on to explain the relationship between deconstruction and philosophy in terms of the search for a radically other "non-site, or non-philosophical site, from which to question philosophy" (108). The hope is that from this non-site, philosophy can appear as an other to itself in order to interrogate itself. Derrida knows well the difficulty, if not sheer impossibility, of such a project, mainly because this non-site that serves as the locus for philosophy's self-reflection and self-interrogation is "radically irreducible to philosophy . . . [and] cannot be defined or situated by means of philosophical language" (108). He restates the problem later in the dialogue:

> It is simply that our belonging to, and inheritance in, the language of metaphysics is something that can only be rigorously and adequately thought about from *another* topos or space where our problematic rapport with the boundary of metaphysics can be seen in a more radical light. Hence my attempts to discover the non-place or *non-lieu* which would be the 'other' of philosophy. This is the task of deconstruction (112).

In this explication of philosophy and deconstruction, in which deconstruction is defined as a search for an other, one can already see a Levinasian paradigm in the background, specifically in the desire for a radical other that interrogates or calls into question.

Derrida, in response to Kearney's questions, asserts the necessity of "an internal critique or deconstruction" (116) in every culture, saying that cultures do not develop without such a critique. Indeed, it is in and through violent, oppositional relationship with an other that identity is established in the first place, whether the identity is that of an individual, nation, or culture. Despite often pervasive illusions of self-sufficiency, every identity is "haunted by its other" (116) and by "traces of an alterity which [refuse] to be totally domesticated" (117). Furthermore,

> the rapport of self-identity is itself always a rapport of violence with the other; so that the notions of property, appropriation and self-presence, so central to logocentric metaphysics, are essentially dependent on an oppositional relation with otherness. In this sense, identity *presupposes* alterity. (117)

Derrida insists, then, upon the importance of the other—or desire for the other—in the project of deconstruction. Indeed, it is desire for the other than assures that deconstruction is not a nihilism, but instead an affirmation of a sort. Derrida flatly denies that deconstruction involves a "suspension of reference" (123), or is synonymous with a nihilism, linguistic or otherwise. He maintains that while deconstruction complicates and problematizes issues of referentiality, it is in no way an assertion that there is nothing outside language; deconstruction, in fact, asserts the opposite:

> Deconstruction is always deeply concerned with the 'other' of language . . . The critique of logocentrism is above all else as search for the 'other' and the 'other of language'. . . . The other, which is beyond language and which summons language, is perhaps not a 'referent' in the normal sense which linguists have attached to this term. But to distance oneself thus from the habitual structure of reference, to challenge or complicate our common assumptions about it, does not amount to saying that there is *nothing* beyond language. (123–4)

The search for the other keeps deconstruction from amounting to a suspension of referentiality; likewise, the desire for the other or, more specifically, the response to the summons of the other disallows the equation of deconstruction with nihilism. In fact, deconstruction includes an affirmation of sorts. Derrida explains:

> I totally refuse the label of nihilism that has been ascribed to me and my American colleagues. Deconstruction is not an enclosure in nothingness, but an openness towards the other. . . . Deconstruction certainly entails a moment of affirmation. Indeed, I cannot conceive of a radical critique which would not be ultimately motivated by some sort of affirmation, acknowledged or not. Deconstruction always presupposes affirmation. . . . I mean that deconstruction is, in itself, a positive response to an alterity which necessarily calls, summons or motivates it. Deconstruction is therefore a vocation—a response to a call. (118, 124)

I argue that there is a resonance between the vocation of deconstruction, as Derrida defines it in the Kearney dialogue, and the religious impetus or sensibility of Dillard as it is exhibited in her nature writing. Derrida uses the term 'vocation' to refer to what I call the 'impulse' of deconstruction *and* of Dillard's work, namely, an openness to and desire for the other. Desire for the other, for Derrida, manifests as a search for the other of philosophy, the search for the non-site at which philosophy can appear as an other to itself. Desire for the other, for Dillard, exhibits itself as the quest for the various tropes and/or representatives of the otherness in nature, i.e. muskrats, amoebas, blood cells, parasites, winds, floods, etc., these entities and forces that are familiar to us and provide the natural backdrop to our lives, but who also harbor violence and mete out destruction. The concealment of an oppositional and violent relation to an other in traditional western identity construction and accounts of representation is what Derrida seeks to expose in his account of *differance* and in his critique of logocentrism. Such critiques, bolstered by a Levinasian ethical sensibility, expose the fact that "representation conceals, while pretending to reveal, the seething turbulence of being . . . its violent underside" (Wyschogrod 1989, 191). Dillard makes an analogous move in her nature writing when she takes a closer than usual look at the allegedly familiar, ultimately benevolent, and useful natural world and finds, instead, a bloodspattered and broken world seething with parasites and disease, a world utterly indifferent in many respects to human needs and desires. Dillard's vision of nature exposes the concealing aspects of sentimentalized and romanticized accounts of the natural world, such as those of the nineteenth century transcendentalists and many contemporary ecologically-minded political theologians. Such accounts sacrifice the call of the other in order to achieve a holistic and useful account of the natural world—holistic in that the instances of destruction and death in nature are taken up and totalized into a larger process of unity and benevolence, useful in the sense that such a rendering of the natural world serves and soothes by offering a benevolent ground upon which to construct models of deity that support certain personal desires and political, social and economic goals. For the sake of a comforting and useful account of the natural world, most reigning politico-theological accounts of nature smooth over and totalize all shreds of otherness, all hints of the universe working *against* human life as much as for it, all hints that the deity modelled upon such a savage world is equally savage. The 'vocation' of Dillard's work in this context is analogous to that of deconstruction in the context of western philosophy: to expose what has been smoothed over, to illumine the 'seething turbulence' and to respond to the call of the 'violent underside'.[11]

My argument for a similar impulse in Dillard's work and in aspects of Derridean deconstruction is analogous to the argument that Stephen Moore makes for a debatable, but nevertheless provocative relationship between deconstruction and Rudolf Bultmann's project of demythologization. Moore suggests that deconstruction is a "reiteration in a new register" of Bultmann's goal in demythologization (150). Moore, in his reading of Bultmann, exploits the radical tendencies of Bultmann's project and determines that deconstruction and demythologization are analogous movements in the history of hermeneutical theory. Moore focuses upon the alienating aspects of demythologization, those aspects that destroy security and deny firm foundations for faith. According to Bultmann, myth is a means by which knowledge of God traditionally is objectified and made useful and foundational for life and faith. Bultmann resists this move and resists myth, calling instead for myth's antithesis: revelation. Revelation, conceived of as an existential encounter and event, offers a challenge to all mythical systems and the comfort they are intended to provide, both epistemologically and salvifically. Revelation, rather than providing certainties about the existence of God or assurances of salvation, actually challenges all such securities and dismantles such mythic systems. Bultmann here aligns himself with a classical Reformed principle of justification by faith alone; mythic systems of security resemble various forms of justification by works in that both afford a certain amount of security and comfort. Bultmann, in *Kerygma and Myth*, claims that demythologization carries the doctrine of justification by faith alone "to its logical conclusion in the field of epistemology" (211). He says:

> Like the doctrine of justification it [demythologization] destroys every false security and every false demand for it on the part of man, whether he seeks it in his good works or in his ascertainable knowledge. The man who wishes to believe in God as his God must realize that he has nothing in his hand on which to base his faith. He is suspended in mid-air, and cannot demand a proof to the Word which addresses him. For the ground and object of faith are identical. Security can be found only by abandoning all security, by being ready, as Luther puts it, to plunge into the inner darkness. (211)

To the extent that myth involves itself in making the strange familiar, offering security and comfort, and in domesticating the eruptive agency of revelation, Bultmann's demythologization is a project analogous to deconstruction in that it points to the self-serving core of such attempts at domestication and securing. Demythologization, in this sense, represents an openness to an other that offers no security, that provides no foundation, and that can in no way be aligned with human culture or desire. Moore reads Bultmann in this way despite the fact that Bultmann's theories of language and of the development of gospel tradition resonate strongly with the ontotheological tradition of which Derridean deconstruction is so critical.

My alignment of Dillard's religious sensibility with the deconstructive impetus is not unlike Moore's alignment of Bultmann's project of demythologization with deconstruction's openness to a destabilizing other. Furthermore, it is possible to discern in the background of such projects of destabilization a Levinasian paradigm, sensibility or, better yet, 'posture', for it is the posture the self takes in regard to the Other that is so crucial in Levinas; moreover, it is this same posturing that Derrida retrieves as a defining feature of deconstruction. Finally, such posture in reference to an Other in nature, an Other metaphorized by nature, a deity modelled upon nature's alterity—such a posture is at the core of Dillard's religious vision. This posture is, however, glaringly absent from the dominant politico-theological accounts of nature and deity, accounts which focus more upon human social and political goals than upon the features of the supposed ground of their theology (nature) that would deny those very goals. Hereby, such accounts, as Thomas á

Kempis claims, show themselves to be mercenary, ever seeking consolations, always thinking of their own profit and advantage. To use McFague's term, such accounts, ironically, are utterly anthropocentric.

Notes

1. So-called 'raw nature' is not the only example of the elemental in Levinas's view. He includes, for example, the city or other such environments which, in their own way perhaps, do not serve a utility or purpose. In the interest of my argument, I will focus on those examples of the elemental that resonate most closely with Dillard's reflections on nature.

2. In the essay "Meaning and Sense," Levinas speaks of the one-way movement as a work. "An orientation which goes *freely* from the Same to the Other is a work . . . A work conceived radically is a movement of the Same towards the Other which never returns to the Same" (Levinas 1987, 91), he says.

3. Important to note here is that Levinas's 'third' is not the Hegelian third that appears in the *Aufhebung*, in the sublation of difference between thesis and antithesis in favor of a third synthesis.

4. In *Otherwise than Being*, Levinas elaborates upon the infinite, saying "The infinite . . . cannot be tracked down like game by a hunter. The trace left by the infinite is not the residue of a presence; its very glow is ambiguous. Otherwise, its positivity would not preserve the infinity of the infinite any more than negativity would" (12).

5. Levinas claims in this essay that the face is not a plastic form, and that it differs from, say, an animal's head because the latter "in its brutish dumbness, is not yet in touch with itself" (55), and the animal is not the master of the meaning it delivers in facial expressions. Yet, Levinas offers the roar of the lion as an example of alterity, which implies a face. Perhaps it's just the roar, not the head, of the lion that signals alterity. On the other hand, who is to say for certain that the faces of animals do not express intended meanings? John Llewelyn discusses some of these issues in his article "Am I Obsessed by Bobby? (Humanism of the Other Animal)" *Re-Reading Levinas*, edited by Robert Bernasconi and Simon Critchley (Bloomington: Indiana University Press, 1991), 234–45.

6. Perhaps Jean-Luc Marion's distinction in *God Without Being* between the idol and the icon is helpful here. The idol and the icon represent "a manner of being for beings" (7), that focuses around the issue of spectatorship. One looks at an idol, but one is looked at by an icon. In other words, in viewing an idol, one is viewing "in order that representation, and hence knowledge can seize hold of it" (10). In relation to the icon, however, "the gaze no longer belongs here to the man . . . [but] to the icon itself . . . the icon regards us" (19). The distinction between idol and icon resides, perhaps, not in them respectively, but in the posture or disposition of the viewer/viewed; in short, whether something is an idol or an icon depends upon one's willingness to be viewed, one's submission to a gaze of the invisible. Similarly, the 'facefulness' of nature or the impersonal gods in Levinas's work may ultimately depend upon the posture of the I toward them, whether or not the I is open to the encounter with the Other.

7. Even as I write this, the Mississippi River has barely returned to its banks after destroying dozens of communities, dams, and levees built along its edges to contain it. The flooding Mississippi resembles the flooding creek Dillard writes about in the middle of

Pilgrim. The creek that had served her, that had seemed manageable and calm, suddenly turned into a raging force that killed livestock and ruined property. The creek that had been so familiar turned into a strange and alien force. She compares it to opening a kitchen drawer and finding a snake.

8. Fritzell points out that for Dillard—or anyone—to talk about such otherness and wildness violates the other and the wild. In this notion he rings Levinasian in that the latter acknowledges that language, being an act of representation, is a kind of violence to the Other. In Derrida's summation, "I could not possibly speak of the Other, make of the Other a theme, pronounce the Other as object, in the accusative. I can only, I *must* only speak to the other . . . in the vocative, which is not a category, a *case* of speech, but, rather the bursting forth, the very raising up of speech" (Derrida 1978, 103).

9. Those theologies which, I argue, require nature and God to submit to their preconceived ideas of justice, goodness, etc., are not unlike the nineteenth-century wilderness explorers who submitted the panoramas of the Rocky Mountains, and others, to European aesthetic standards that required specific foregrounds to be considered truly artistic. These explorers (tourists), according to Paul T. Bryant, "impos[ed] the criteria of art upon the perception of nature"; he adds sarcastically that "somehow nature in northern Colorado overlooked this important [criteria]" (24). He argues that those who see nature as one sees a picture ultimately seek to control nature and use it for their own purposes, in this case, aesthetic ones. Such a stance is opposed by those who envision nature as a milieu in which one lives, as the arena of action. Bryant argues that "the most informed nature writing typically presents nature as milieu" (33). Ironically, according to this definition, Levinas, who in no way claims to be a nature writer, may perhaps be more of a nature writer than McFague, who specifically describes herself as writing a theology rooted in nature. See Paul T. Bryant, "Nature as Picture/Nature as Milieu," *The CEA Critic: An Official Journal of the College English Association* 54 (Fall 1991): 22–33.

10. See Taylor's *Nots*, 10–95; Jacques Derrida, "How to Avoid Speaking: Denials," *Languages of the Unsayable: The Play of Negativity in Literature and Literary Theory*, ed. Sanford Budick and Wolfgang Iser (New York: Columbia University Press, 1989), 3–70.

11. Dillard's vision of the brokenness and turbulence in the natural world and its eruption of sentimental and holistic accounts is similar to Taylor's explication of disease in relation to the body. Against the "romantic notion of the organism advanced by nineteenth-century artists and poets," in which health is the given and disease an accident from outside, Taylor suggests a postmodern view of the body which sees disease or fault as "not secondary or accidental but [as] necessary to the constitution of the system as such . . . Disease arises as if from within to disrupt an equilibrium or harmony that was never present in the first place" (Taylor 1993, 236).

Chapter 5

God and the Critiques of Religion

> It is this comfortable belief—that the purposes of the Almighty coincide with our purely human purposes—that religious faith requires us to renounce.
> —Christopher Lasch

In the last few decades, feminist theology has established itself as a vital discipline within the larger arena of the study of religion. The importance and enduring power of the many feminist approaches to the study of religions and religious thought are due, at least partially, to the role that feminist studies in religion has taken on at different times in its history: that of critique. Feminist work in religion has illumined many features of religious history and thought that went unnoticed or were deemed unimportant, specifically those historical events or ideas connected in some way to women. This work, however—and other work like it—is done with the assumption that feminist approaches to religion are first and foremost a critique of the traditional ways of doing theology and religious study. Feminist approaches expose the patriarchal, oppressive, and reductionistic methods of inquiry embedded in traditional Western accounts of religious history, thought, and culture, and the ways in which women's experience and existence are routinely left out of deliberations on the nature of God, the sacred, and other discussion proper to religious study. Feminist history uncovers the hidden histories of women that have been buried under centuries of androcentric chronicling and, in doing so, excoriates traditional historical methods for their sexism and oppression. This kind of study in religion has contributed greatly to the field by serving as a critique of traditional methodologies and presuppositions; furthermore, with this critique in the background, feminists have set out not only to reform, but fundamentally to reshape religious thought and study in a way that does not betray the experiences of women and their contributions to the field of study.

Given the importance of critique in a feminist approach to any discipline, it is surprising that the most widely received feminist accounts of God or the sacred give virtually no time to defending their work against some of the most powerful critiques ever wielded against religion in general, specifically those offered by Ludwig Feuerbach, Sigmund Freud and Friedrich Nietzsche. These critiques were and are watershed events in religious thought and any theologian who wishes to contribute to the larger contemporary intellectual climate must come to terms with or at least address the charges brought against traditional Jewish and Christian thought by these thinkers. Feuerbach, Freud and Nietzsche are pertinent here for three reasons: first, the historical significance of their arguments; second, the ways in which these critiques seriously call into question much recent feminist theologizing, and political theologizing in general; finally, the ways in which a Dillardian model of deity, informed by a Levinasian sensitivity to otherness, escapes many of their critiques. Indeed, I see the Dillardian model actually joining Freud, Feuerbach, and Nietzsche in many of their charges against traditional western religion, including recent political theologies.

Of course the assumption behind the last statement is that the feminist models of deity of which I speak in this work, those the Dillardian model challenges, are in some significant way not unlike traditional western conceptions of deity. This is surely a contested assumption because a hallmark of the McFaguean feminist reworking of conceptions of deity—and of religion in general—is that it severely criticizes traditional western models of God. Models of deity that reject notions of hierarchy, fatherhood, and domination and focus instead upon the feminine and the organic can certainly be said to be a deviation from traditional western concepts of deity, at least as far as they go. Important, however, are the ways in which McFague's models, for example, and those of traditional western Christian theology remain fundamentally similar. In both sets of models, God or deity interacts with human history and even individual human lives. While in McFague's view, God does not intervene to interrupt natural forces or even evil human forces, God is still somehow "on the side of" those who are oppressed and broken in human history. God is still good for McFague in much the same way that God's ultimate goodness is uncontested in traditional western thinking. God the Mother, Lover, and Friend does not differ much, in this respect, from God the benevolent Father and Ruler of all creation. In both scenarios, God is seen as being on the side of— if not the guarantor—of goodness, order, justice, and human spiritual and moral development. The fundamental attributes of deity in the McFaguean view do not change significantly from those advanced by traditional western theology; what changes are the images and models used to represent the bearer of these attributes. Granted, maleness is replaced with femaleness, hierarchy with solidarity, punishment with nurturance; however the underlying assumption of both views is that God is good, the foundation of justice, and supportive of human well-being.[1]

These are exactly the features of Western religion and of its conception of deity that Feuerbach and Freud challenge so thoroughly. Feuerbach and Freud call into question the existence of the ultimately benevolent, powerful, and moral deity of western theology, of which McFague's theology is a later example. God the Mother, Lover, and Friend does not escape this critique any more than God the Father, Lord, and Judge (or Father, Son, and Holy Ghost); therefore, this chapter is devoted to the Feuerbachian/Freudian and the Nietzschean critiques of religion and their bearing upon contemporary feminist models of deity as opposed to models gleaned from my reading of Dillard.

The Feuerbachian Critique of Religion

According to Eugene Kamenka, religion for Feuerbach was "the fundamental phenomenon in the history of human culture; to understand it was to understand man. It was for this reason that Feuerbach was anxious to deny that he was an atheist: he had not come to destroy religion, but to explain it" (35). Feuerbach argued that the real root of religious belief was not the objective existence of the object of worship, such as a deity; instead, the impetus for religious worship and belief lies in human need and feelings of dependence, and the projection of human desires for life in the empirical, natural world. In other words, according to Feuerbach in *The Essence of Christianity*, "the 'Divine Being' is nothing else than the nature of Man, i.e., human nature purified, freed from the imperfections of the human individual, projected onto the outside, and viewed and revered as a different and distinct being with a nature of its own. All the attributes of the 'Divine Being' are therefore attributes of man" (Feuerbach 1957, 12). Humans find what is desirable in and good for themselves and society, and separate these positive attributes from the human and assign them to an outside entity, a deity, and then worship that deity as a distinct being. God becomes the repository for desirable human qualities such as goodness, patience, love, as well as for those things humans desire for society at large, such as moral standards and codes of justice. Furthermore, God becomes the one who protects and saves, which, according to Feuerbach, is an expression of the alienation, dependence, and fear humans feel in regard to nature. Feuerbach's critique of religion in *The Essence of Christianity*, then, while greatly influential in its own day and still popular today, is a position and work "whose substance and whose leading idea is simple and even ancient: that man created the Gods and that the Gods embody man's own conception of his own humanity, his own wishes, fears, needs, and ideals" (Wartofsky 1977, 197).

Kamenka notes that readers of Feuerbach should not take him too literally when he speaks of the 'essence' of religion which "according to Feuerbach, is sometimes man, sometimes love, sometimes dependence, sometimes nature, and so on" (56). Kamenka suggests that rather than presenting any one of these as the absolute essence of religion, Feuerbach's analysis of religion shows that these different aspects of religion are part of a "complex social phenomenon" (56), and that they operate together in relations of mutual dependence. Thus, the particular aspect of religion that Feuerbach will, at a given time, identify as its essence will depend upon what strand of religious dogma or what feature of a religious worldview Feuerbach is studying at that time. While most religious doctrines can be boiled down to a wish of some sort, the object of that wish changes from dogma to dogma. For example, Feuerbach argues that behind the fundamental Christian doctrine of a Redeemer lies "the desire to be freed from moral evils instantaneously, immediately, and by a stroke of magic, that is in an absolutely subjective, easy way" (Feuerbach 1957, 41). Behind the doctrine of personal immortality is discerned human desire to "directly claim for their own individual selves what belongs only to the totality of the species" (46). The belief in Christ's resurrection is the result of "man's desire for the immediate certainty of his personal existence after death. Christ's resurrection proves personal immortality to be an unquestionable fact" (38). The doctrine of creation, both Jewish and Christian, expresses the desire to control nature and have it serve human purposes; furthermore, it "is an expression of egotism and possible only when man feels himself no longer a part of Nature" (34).

These examples give an indication of the kind of treatment Feuerbach gives various fundamental religious beliefs, although I cannot enter here into the complexities of his argumentation. What concerns my argument here is the way in which Feuerbach treats nature and the human relation to nature in the construction of religion. I have touched upon human egotism in regard to nature; now I will focus upon this theme in Feuerbach to make my points about the benevolent deities of much contemporary political theology.

In lecture twelve of his *Lectures on the Essence of Religion*, Feuerbach discusses one of the most important proofs for God's existence in western traditional religion: the cosmological proof. He denies the validity of this proof on the grounds that it does not solve the difficulties it claims to solve. Nature is complex and exhibits a multitude of causes and effects, and cannot be explained in terms of one single cause, such as a deity, that exists outside nature. Furthermore, he claims, there is nothing to prevent one, once one has posited an outside deity as the first and only cause of the natural world, from going beyond this alleged first cause to seek for a cause and ground of God. Finally, Feuerbach claims that there exists no cause without an effect; if the effect is omitted, the cause disappears as well. Cause and effect are dependent upon each other for their respective existences. God as First Cause, then, cannot retain the status of being a deity outside and independent of nature, because God as Cause depends upon nature as effect for existence. "Thus," Feuerbach concludes, "the difficulties arising from the beginning of the world are not only postponed or thrust aside or glossed over by the notion of a God, a being outside the world; they are *not solved*" (101). A key phrase in this sentence is "a being outside the world," for it is the existence of this being that Feuerbach attacks.

Feuerbach claims that "our world—not only our political and social world, but our learned, intellectual world as well—is a world upside down" (103). It is upside down in the sense that what are deemed to be prior are actually derivative; what is considered to be first can be proven actually to be last. This is true of God and nature. While the cosmological proof of God's existence asserts that the existence of nature presupposes the existence of its prior cause, namely, God, Feuerbach asserts the opposite. God, an infinite being, did not exist first to then cause nature; nature exists infinitely and leads to the positing of God. This movement is seen, Feuerbach maintains, most clearly in the fact that the characteristics and attributes of God that are not borrowed from man—like justice, love, etc.—are those seen in nature, specifically power, sustenance, beauty, infinity, and vastness. The effects of nature are effects which humans cannot produce, thus reinforcing human limitation. These effects of nature become "the model from which man originally derive[s] the notion and concept of a superhuman divine power" (105–6). The predicates of God, such as power, infinity, and eternity are originally predicates of nature which are then abstracted from nature and ascribed to a superhuman, supernatural divine being who is determined to be the *cause* and *originator* of nature, so that "nature disappear[s] behind God" (108). Thus, for Feuerbach, the world is upside down; while it is claimed that God is the origin of the magnificent natural world, actually the natural world is the origin of God.

Moreover, Feuerbach claims, not only are God's power, eternity, infinity, etc., derived from nature, so are his moral attributes. In the thirteenth lecture, he states that "God's goodness is merely abstracted from those beings and phenomena in nature which are useful, good and helpful to man, which give him the feeling or consciousness that life, existence, is a good thing, a blessing" (111). Evil gods or angry gods are posited when nature is not kind or helpful to humans. While the polytheist may posit good gods and evil gods, the monotheist replaces these various gods with one God who is both good and evil. The evil in the one God, however, is often interpreted as anger, more specifically, punitive anger against injustice. Feuerbach explains:

> [The monotheist] believes in one God, but this one God is a good *and* evil, or angry, God, a God with conflicting attributes. But God's wrath is nothing more than His *punitive justice* looked upon as an affect of passion. Anger is also a basic trait in man; essentially it is nothing else than a passionate desire for justice or vengeance. Man becomes angry when . . . a wrong, an injustice, has been done to him. Anger is a man's revolt against the despotic encroachment of another being. Just as God's goodness is originally derived from the good effects of nature, so justice is originally derived from its harmful, destructive effects. Man is an egoist; he is infinitely fond of himself, he believes that all things exist for his sole benefit and that there neither should or can be evils. But he runs into facts that conflict with this self-centered faith; he therefore supposes that evil befalls him only when he transgresses against the being or beings from whom he derives everything that is good and helpful, so arousing their anger. He explains the evils of nature as punishments that God metes out to man because of some transgression or injustice committed against Him. (112)

In this passage, we see the mechanism by which humans ascribe to deity what they wish for themselves. As Feuerbach asserts, a central human desire is for justice and goodness in life, and when this desire is thwarted, anger wells up. This human desire for justice, then, is projected onto God so that human actions can be measured against a divine, allegedly prior standard of justice, and the events of nature that offend human self-interest can be interpreted as God's acts of punitive justice. Behind such mechanisms and maneuvers of deity construction is human egoism, an egoism that resists and resents the "despotic encroachments" of any human being or any entity in nature. When such encroachments occur, on the part of humans or nature, the religious system is in place to account for these encroachments in ways that maintain the right and claim of humanity for a good, blessed life.

Such egoism is the hallmark of the type of religion Feuerbach critiques. In the fifth lecture, Feuerbach distinguishes this egoistic faith from the type of religion that he himself claims to profess, namely, a nature religion. He is careful, however, to elucidate the specific kind of nature religion with which he finds affinity. On the one hand, there is religion that has become synonymous with western theology, the egoistic religion that abstracts from nature a deity who then turns around and claims responsibility for all that exists. This kind of religion, Feuerbach claims,

> has wrenched man out of his relationship with the world, isolated him, made him into an arrogant self-centered being who exalts himself above nature . . . it is only against this arrogant, presumptuous ecclesiastical religion, which, being ecclesiastical, is now represented by a special official class, that I take up cudgels. (35)

On the other hand, there is ancient nature religion which, although he identifies himself with it, often holds a feature he must reject, namely, superstition. He explains:

> [E]ven though I identify my view with nature religion, I must ask you to remember that even nature religion contains an element which I reject. For although, as the name itself indicates, the object of nature religion is nature and nothing else, nevertheless, to man in his earliest stage, that of nature religion, nature is not an object as it is in reality, but is only what it seems to his uncultivated and inexperienced reason, to his imagination and feeling. Even here, accordingly, man has supernatural desires and consequently makes supernatural—or what amounts to the same thing—unnatural demands upon nature. Or to put it differently and more clearly: not even nature religion is free of superstition, for in their natural state, that is, without education and experience, all men, as Spinoza recognized, are subject to superstition. And when I speak in favor of nature religion, I do not wish to be suspected of also favoring religious superstition. (36–7)

Feuerbach, apparently, is speaking of a strict pantheism that imagines the various effects of nature—trees, rocks, rivers—to be actual entities or even deities to whom one might appeal for favors through various rituals. The superstition that he speaks of here is a mechanism by which human desires—amplified by emotion and imagination—are projected onto the effects of nature and become, perhaps, personified, but not distinct and abstracted from nature as in the egoistic religion described above. So, these two religious varieties—egoistic philosophical religion and superstitious nature religion—become two extremes that Feuerbach wishes to avoid when explaining his own religious position as an atheist. He seeks, instead, to avoid "the superlatives or exaggerations of religious emotion," and to "take things as they are, to make *no more*, but *also no less* of them than they are. Nature religion, pantheism, makes too much of nature, while conversely, idealism, theism, Christianity make too little of it, and indeed ignore it" (37). Feuerbach explains what he determines to be the middle ground and, thus, his own religious position:

> I hate the idealism that wrenches man out of nature; I am not ashamed of my dependency on nature; I openly confess that the workings of nature affect not only my surface, my skin, my body, but also my core, my innermost being. . . . I do not, like a Christian, believe that such a dependence is contrary to my true being or hope to be delivered from it. I know further that I am a finite mortal being, that I shall one day cease to exist. But I find this *very natural* and am therefore perfectly reconciled to the thought. . . . In nature religion I recognize neither more nor less that what I recognize in all religion, including the Christian, namely, *its simple fundamental truth*. And this truth is only that man is dependent upon nature, that he should live in harmony with nature, that even in his highest intellectual development he should not forget that he is a part and child of nature, but at all times honor nature and hold it sacred, not only as the ground and source of his existence, but also as the ground and source of his mental and physical wellbeing, for it is only through nature that man can become free of all morbidly excessive demands and desires, such as the desire for immortality. (35, 37)

In many important respects, the dominant religious vision of current American feminist theology resonates with the nature religion with which Feuerbach aligns himself in the above passage. As explained in the introduction to this work, feminist theology has taken as one of its chief goals the task of reconceiving the human/ earth relationship in terms that are more friendly and respectful of the natural world. Accomplishing this has involved rethinking and re-theologizing dominant Jewish and Christian conceptions of deity *away* from a view of severe separation between God and the world, in which the two are utterly opposed to each other, and *toward* a view of fundamental relation between deity and the earth, in which the two embody and are expressive of each other in important ways. Many feminists have tried to avoid, without specific reference to Feuerbach, the two extremes that he seeks to avoid in his *Lectures*, namely, anthropocentric religion and pantheism. McFague, for example, offers a revision of traditional Christian religion that replaces the hierarchically superior and abstract God manifested in the Father, Son, and Holy Ghost with a fundamentally this-worldly deity who exists in mutual relation with all beings, and who is manifested most clearly as a Mother, Lover, and Friend who has the earth as her body. Indeed, such theological revisions are substantial correctives against much of the selfishness that characterizes traditional western religion with regard to nature, at least as Feuerbach describes it. In this way, feminist revisionist theologies can be said to exempt themselves from the Feuerbachian critique of religion, having themselves attempted to reconfigure the human/nature and nature/deity relationship in a similar fashion.

Feminist theological revisions, however, have failed to root out an important strand of anthropocentrism despite their attempts at removing it from the western religious vision. Granted, they admit that humans are not the center of the cosmos. They acknowledge that humans are but one species among many, all of whom have equal claim to life on the planet. They even conceive of deity in a way that allows for very little, if any, divine intervention into the laws of nature, so that one might be spared from natural tragedy. This same deity, however, while modelled upon nature, *still retains human social and political goals as her concern*; in this respect, feminist models remain anthropocentric and egoistic. Furthermore, to posit such a deity that is at once modelled upon the natural world—a world both supportive of and hostile to human existence—*and* is at the same time intimately concerned with the plight of the oppressed peoples of the world is an utter contradiction. To continually maintain divine concern for injustices in the world when insisting upon modelling deity upon the natural world is to cling quite tenaciously to the hope for a God who makes all things right, who makes "rough places plain," and who vindicates the oppressed in the end. Such a deity, as Feuerbach shows, is a human construction behind which lies the human desire for things to operate in a way that ultimately serves human purposes.

This strand of anthropocentrism remaining in feminist revisionist theologies is, however, absent in Dillard's work. Dillard's religious vision, like that of many feminists, relies upon nature as the ground for theologizing or speaking about deity. Furthermore, influenced as she is by contemporary scientific understandings of the human/earth relationship, Dillard maintains a nonanthropocentric vision of the world throughout her work in the sense that she realizes that the human is only one species among millions. In this, too, she joins many feminist theologians. What distinguishes Dillard from revisionist feminist theologies, however, is that at no point in her work is there even the hint that the deity modelled upon nature's expansiveness, beauty, and violence is concerned with human political, social, and/or economic goals. Dillard's world is utterly theocentric, not anthropocentric. It is theocentric because it operates in accordance with its own often mysterious interests, not in accordance with the goals of human cultural or moral development. Therefore, when a natural disaster occurs, commonly and with good reason called an "act of God," and thousands of oppressed people are killed, regardless of their struggles for equality or representation or freedom, those of the Dillardian view will grieve along with everyone else, but they will not be thrown into theological conflict. The Dillardian view does not presume to domesticate the wild-eyed deity of the natural world, nor does it assume that human interests are privileged interests among the many species that live on the earth. Despite the assertions to the contrary, the dominant feminist theologies do presume and assume these things and, thus, remain ultimately anthropocentric.

Therefore, with regard to the Feuerbachian critique of traditional western religion, it seems that the Dillardian religious vision and the models of deity contained therein not only survive the critique, but comply with its provisions in important ways. In other words, I have argued in this work that the Dillardian religious vision offers a critique of the dominant feminist theologies in contemporary American thought. I hope to have shown that Dillard's critique and alternative religious vision is of a piece with that of Feuerbach in that both approaches take the natural world as the ground for religion, relying upon the given, material, real world rather than any transcendent, abstracted ideal or any projected, personified wish or desire for how one might want the world to be. Dominant feminist theologies fail because they have as their root not an honest look at the empirical reality of nature and its cruelty, but a sentimentalized hope for a nature and deity that loves, heals, and nurtures exclusively—in short, an idealized human that is not sexist, hierarchical, dominating, or patriarchal.

The Freudian Critique of Religion

Peter Gay notes that while a student in Vienna, Freud wrote of Ludwig Feuerbach: "Among all philosophers I worship and admire this man the most" (53). While Feuerbach lost some of his pull on the older Freud, Feuerbach's influence can still be seen in Freud's work, especially in his critique and analysis of religion. Not only did Freud continue in the stylistic tradition of Feuerbach, a tradition opposed to the abstractions and obscurities typical of German academic prose, he also insisted upon, even more vehemently than Feuerbach, the materialism and adherence to the scientific worldview that Feuerbach maintained throughout his work. Freud's conviction of the animosity between science and religion will be discussed later; for now, let us focus on Freud's distinctive continuation of Feuerbach's argument that religion is rooted in wish-fulfillment. Freud's most direct confrontation with traditional western religion comes in his *The Future of an Illusion*, published initially in 1927. I will use it exclusively in this discussion despite the fact that Freud elaborates some of the themes found in it elsewhere in his work, specifically in *Totem and Taboo, Civilization and its Discontents*, and *Moses and Monotheism.*[2]

Early in *The Future of an Illusion*, Freud identifies two observable aspects of human civilization: knowledge of and the capacity to control nature, and all regulations needed to govern human relations (5–6). Despite humanity's hostility to civilization because of the burdens and restrictions it places upon human instincts (an idea Freud develops later), civilization is necessary primarily to defend against nature. Civilization, while hard to bear, is not as exacting as nature. Freud explains:

It is true that nature would not demand any restrictions of instinct from us, she
would let us do as we liked; but she has her own particularly effective method of
restricting us. She destroys us—coldly, cruelly, relentlessly, as it seems to us, and
possibly through the very things that occasioned our satisfaction. It was precisely
because of these dangers with which nature threatens us that we came together
and created civilization, which is also, among other things, intended to make our
communal life possible. For the principal task of civilization, its actual *raison
d'etre*, is to defend us against nature. (15)

Freud goes on:

But no one is under the illusion that nature has already been vanquished; and few
dare hope that she will ever be entirely subjected to man. There are the elements,
which seem to mock at all human control: the earth, which quakes and is torn
apart and buries all human life and its works; water, which deluges and drowns
everything in a turmoil; storms, which blow everything before them; there are
diseases, which we have only recently recognized as attacks from other organisms;
and finally there is the painful riddle of death, against which no medicine has yet
been found, nor probably will be. With these forces nature rises up against us,
majestic, cruel and inexorable; she brings to our mind once more our weakness
and helplessness, which we thought to escape through the work of civilization.
(15–6)

I quote Freud at length here not only to get us to the point of discussing his
theory of the role of wish-fulfillment in the development of religion, but to point
out his acute sense of the cruel realities of nature which, of course, is a central
theme in this work. Little editing would be required to lift Freud's words quoted
above and transport them to any of several of Dillard's works, so similar in tone
are their accounts of nature. According to Freud, it is against this majestic and
horrific vision of nature that humans construct a civilization, even though that
very civilization "imposes some amount of privation on [them], and other men
bring [them] a measure of suffering, either in spite of the precepts of [their]
civilization or because of its imperfections" (16). The compilation of hardships
brought on by civilization and the threats to human existence from nature
fundamentally attack humanity's "natural narcissism" and "result in a permanent
state of anxious expectation" (16). In short,

Man's self-regard, seriously menaced, calls for consolation; life and the universe
must be robbed of their terrors; moreover, his curiosity, moved, it is true, by the
strongest practical interest, demands an answer. (16)

As Freud will argue, religion is a most tenacious part of that answer.[3]
    The first and most substantial step toward alleviating human anxiety in the
face of nature and civilization's hardships is to humanize nature. Humans ascribe
to nature some measure of personhood, so that tragedies of nature become the acts

of a Will, and the forces that destroy become emotions of a Being. By humanizing the forces of nature, we "can feel at home in the uncanny and can deal by psychical means with our senseless anxiety" (17). Moreover, we can appeal to nature and the beings therein; "we can try to adjure them, to appease them, to bribe them, and, by so influencing them, we may rob them of a part of their power" (17). The movement by which humans turn nature into gods has an infantile prototype. It is nothing short of a reenactment of the relationship the child constructs in relation to the father, a relationship of helplessness, fear, and, hopefully, trust acquired through various influences. Therefore, it is no surprise to Freud that the dominant images of deity in western religion privilege maleness and fatherhood (17, 19, 23–4).

The humanization of nature, then, begins the movement wherein is created

> a store of ideas . . . born from man's need to make his helplessness tolerable and built up from the material of memories of the helplessness of his own childhood and the childhood of the human race. It can clearly be seen that the possession of these ideas protects him in two directions—against the dangers of nature and Fate, and against the injuries that threaten him from society itself. (18)

Contained in this store of ideas are notions that: life's purpose is to perfect human nature; a superior intelligence "orders everything for the best—that is, to make it enjoyable for us" (19); "a benevolent Providence" watches over us "which is only seemingly stern and which will not suffer us to become a plaything of the overmighty and pitiless forces of nature" (19); death is not an end, but a new beginning; civilization's moral laws are, in fact, those of the divine; good is rewarded and evil is punished, and so on. The deepest of human desires—to be protected from the evils of nature and society—account for the construction of religious systems, systems which have at their core what Freud calls humanity's "natural narcissism." Deity, in such systems, resembles a parent or father who, although sometimes stern and angry, ultimately has human well-being and concerns as his own, and will not allow society or nature to significantly or in any ultimate sense ravage the human social, moral order. The belief in such a deity, according to Freud, is an illusion, primarily because "a wish-fulfillment is a prominent factor in its motivation" (31).

In Freud's understanding, humanity is more deeply attached to religious systems than to any other institution or endeavor in society. Religious ideas, he says,

> are prized as the most precious possession of civilization, as the most precious thing it has to offer its participants. It is far more highly prized than all the devices for winning treasures from the earth or providing men with sustenance or preventing their illnesses, and so forth. People feel that life would not be tolerable if they did not attach to these ideas the value that is claimed for them. (20)

Here, one gets a hint at Freud's uncompromising belief in the animosity between religion and science. Peter Gay notes the late nineteenth- and early twentieth-century

European intellectual climate into which Freud was born and developed his work. Books like Draper's *History of the Conflict between Religion and Science* and White's *History of the Warfare of Science with Theology in Christendom* were immensely popular in the nineteenth century and, as Gay explains, "encapsulate, in their incendiary titles, a deeply felt nineteenth-century perception" (6). Gay observes that figures such as William James and Ernst Haeckel suggested that nineteenth-century individuals maintained a division in their minds between religious thought and belief, on the one hand, and scientific understanding on the other. This division itself indicates an incommensurability between religion and science that, according to Gay, was never overcome regardless of various truces and compromises made on either side. "[S]izable pockets of anticlericalism and of secularist contempt for all religion were scattered across the map of European culture, " (7) Gay explains, and it was into this terrain that Freud worked out psychoanalytic theory and developed his views of religion.

Freud, however, was perhaps more radical in his belief that religion was the enemy of science. Even writers who asserted the incompatibility of Christianity with science, such as Draper and White, suggested ways in which one might negotiate the two into a compromise. Gay writes:

> Arm in arm with Draper, White postulated a God of some sort and stood, hat reverently in hand, before the glorious mysteries of the universe. Like so many among the nineteenth-century troop carrying the banner of the enlightenment, liberalism, and science, he and Draper were pervaded by the oceanic feeling of awe before the universe that Freud could not detect in himself. They cherished that undefinable sense of connectedness which Freud's acquaintance Rolland Romain took to be at the heart of religious sentiments. Freud professed an interest in analyzing that feeling but he did not really respect it. It smacked of nonalcoholic apple juice working, like an undetected placebo, to induce a state of religious intoxication. For Freud, to be scientific meant to be sober. (16–7)

A significant part of this "sobriety" for Freud is intellectual honesty, and it is the absence of this feature in religious thinking that most offends Freud, thus prompting him to write: "Where questions of religion are concerned, people are guilty of every sort of dishonesty and intellectual misdemeanor" (32). Therefore, religion is the enemy of science for Freud because of its tenacious, even neurotic hold onto illusory beliefs that have as their origins *not* the clearminded operations of reason and science, but the deeply-imbedded desires for consolation in a world that is often hostile and repressive. The strength of these illusory beliefs is illustrated in the mental gymnastics performed to maintain them in the face of glaring opposition from reality, reason, and scientific achievement.[4]

I have focused here upon two specific aspects of Freud's critique of religion— the location of religious belief in wish fulfillment, and the animosity between religion and science—in order to draw as sharply as possible the ways in which I think the Dillardian religious vision and the models of deity therein actually complement the Freudian critique, *and* to illumine ways in which dominant feminist theologies fall short in terms of surviving the critique. On the issue of wish fulfillment, it seems clear that what I argued earlier in the Feuerbach section remains true here, namely, that the dominant feminist models of deity can easily be traced to a deeply held desire for a God who consoles, who supports human endeavors, and who shares human ideas about justice and suffering. Furthermore, because the Dillardian model of deity in no way responds to desires for consolation, but rather highlights the otherness and indifference of deity/nature, it therefore cannot be dismissed as an illusory belief. One who shares Dillard's perspective knows that the power of/in the universe is not unqualifiedly on the side of human life and endeavor, that the stores of consolation and security run short quite often here in the harsh and exacting world and, finally, that death often appears the given and life the exception in a human existence that lasts only a moment before it is "plowed under" like everything else to become food for the next crop. Such a religious vision in no way resembles that which Freud mercilessly criticizes in *The Future of an Illusion*; however, it does resemble the "education to reality" Freud champions at the end of the book.

In section nine, Freud argues with his imaginary opponent over the necessity of consolation in life. His opponent charges that Freud is naive to think that humans can live without the consolations given by religious belief. Freud disagrees. He allows that it would be impossible and even cruel to strip religious belief from people who have from their earliest moments been trained within its parameters. He compares such an attempt to that of taking sleeping pills away from someone who has relied upon them for most of his life. People, however, do not have to be raised addicted to narcotics or to religious consolations. Freud explains:

> Thus I must contradict you when you go on to argue that men are completely unable to do without the consolation of the religious illusion, that without it they could not bear the troubles of life and the cruelties of reality. That is true, certainly, of the men into whom you have instilled the sweet—or bitter-sweet—poison from childhood onwards. But what of the other men, who have been sensibly brought up? Perhaps those who do not suffer from the neurosis will need no intoxicant to deaden it. They will, it is true, find themselves in a difficult situation. They will have to admit their helplessness and their insignificance in the machinery of the universe; they can no longer be the centre of creation, no longer the object of tender care on the part of a beneficent Providence. They will be in the same position as a child who has left the parental house where he was so warm and comfortable. But surely infantilism is destined to be surmounted. Men cannot remain children forever; they must in the end go out into 'hostile life'. We may call this 'education to reality'. Need I confess to you that the sole purpose of my book is to point out the necessity for this forward step? (49)

I do not overstate when I say that the most important theological point of Dillard's books is to "educate in reality," to take an honest look at "hostile life" and to temper herself and her conceptions of deity against the edges of her vision of violence and beauty intertwined. In this way, she is complicit with Freud in criticizing any religious vision rooted in divine consolation, for inherent in such views are not only desires for something that does not exist, but also the mental machinery to think and act as if it does exist, in short, to think and act dishonestly. Furthermore, Dillard's persona in her work appears to be a prime example of one who survives quite well without the consolations of traditional religion. She begins with harsh realities of the natural world, and then moves on to live within them rather than to explain them away. Dillardian religion, in Freudian terms, becomes that which shakes loose neurotic, anthropocentric religion and forces people to grow up.

Admittedly, Freud may have disagreed. It is probable that his hostility toward religion was so virulent that it prohibited him from conceiving of religion in any other way than he did, namely, as a system of repression and compensation. Freud suggests that a nonanthropocentric religious vision will lose its hold on human interest (54). Furthermore, Rieff suggests that "Freud conceived of no God not originally mortal, none that did not incarnate the human craving for authority— just as in the social sphere he could conceive of no political unity based on anything other than erotic attachment to a personal leader" (264). Dillard's religious vision is one that bypasses the "human craving for authority" and the desire for consolation, yet it maintains its hold because of the possibilities for beauty in viewing the natural world *as it is*, not as one might want it to be. One might say that beauty here is a type of consolation, but it seems that it differs qualitatively and functionally from the consolation of which Freud speaks as being at the center of traditional western religion. Therefore, by aligning Dillard with Freud, I am careful not to overlook the ways in which I think the Dillardian view serves as a corrective to the Freudian. Freud's conception of religion is reductionistic and his scientific "solution" to religious neurosis is positivistic. The Dillardian/Levinasian perspective as I have laid it out moves beyond the Freudian critique in that it wholly embraces a contemporary scientific perspective while maintaining a religious sensibility *not* contradictory to that scientific perspective, and *not* rooted in consolation and wish fulfillment.

Dominant feminist models of deity, however, retain the feature of divine consolation despite the attempt of those who conceive of these models to root them in human experience and knowledge of the natural world, a world which is as antagonistic as it is sustaining. Western feminist theologies, burdened by environmental concerns and the ways human treatment of the earth translates into treatment of women, have revised conceptions of deity away from the anthropocentrism of traditional theology and have focused, instead, upon the interrelation between all species on earth, including the human. Bearing in mind the mutual interdependence of all life forms on earth, feminist theologies have attempted not only to remove the human race from its pedestal as rulers of the earth, but also to remove the pedestal itself. In short, feminist revisionist theologies have tried to do away with the binary thinking that would privilege humans over nature, spirit over matter, men over women, and deity over it all. In this move, they receive what Freud above calls "education to reality" in that they theologize in accordance with a current scientific worldview of interdependence and mutual relation, a worldview opposed to anthropocentrism; however, their education stops here. While they realize, with Freud, that "they can no longer be the centre of creation," they still hope to be "the object of tender care on the part of a beneficent Providence." As pointed out earlier, God the mother, lover, and friend of much dominant feminist religious thought is of a piece with God the father, ruler, and judge in that both are conceived of in fundamentally anthropocentric terms; the former concerns herself with the social, political, and economic well-being of oppressed groups while the latter concerns himself with the blood redemption or spiritual salvation of the human race. Though differing in their specific concerns, both deities are concerned primarily with the human plight. Both religious visions remain infantile in that neither comes to terms with "hostile life" and hopes, instead, for an escape from the harsh realities of human existence. Of course, I am not saying that political, social, or economic oppression is something one should just passively accept as a harsh condition of life; such oppression is of human construction and can and even should be redressed. What I am saying is that such a project cannot have as its ethical, theological foundation a deity who shares in the suffering of the oppressed and who is in solidarity with their liberators, *especially* if this deity is modelled upon the natural world. An honest look at nature does not reveal such a deity; "education to reality" in Freud's terms insists upon such honesty. In dominant feminist theologies, the desire for consolation overrides the initially honest attempt to resist anthropocentrism, resulting in a retention of the very feature of religion that discredits it in Freud's view.

A benevolent deity concerned with the plight of the oppressed offers not only consolation, but also ethical grounding for resistance to oppression. Feminist theologians may argue that such a conception of deity is necessary as the foundation upon which resistance to patriarchal oppression is based; otherwise, such resistance movements lose their ethical drive, their claim to justice. Indeed, a significant ramification of the religious vision I glean from my reading of Dillard is that deity is removed as the ground of human ethical actions. A deity who deals in violence and savagery cannot serve as an ethical model for human society. Dillard's religious vision, then, can be seen as a kind of antifoundationalism in that it does not retain a primary grounding aspect of theological ethics, namely, the ultimate goodness of God conceived of in terms of what is good for humans. The burden for ethics is removed from the shoulders of deity and placed squarely upon those of people, a transference that broadly aligns Dillard's work with that of any number of other nonfoundationalist ethical thinkers, from Epicurus to Hume to Sartre. More specifically, the ethical dimension of Dillard's religious vision is focused almost exclusively upon the human stance toward deity, in its refusal to tame or reduce deity (and nature) to slave status. In this sense, her religious vision can serve as an ethical sensibility that may itself ground various attempts to construct workable and just ethical systems. Granted, the challenge to build ethical systems in an antifoundationalist and/or postmodernist milieu is a formidable one; however, I have also tried to show above that Dillard's perspective, inasmuch as it can be seen through the veil of a Levinasian ethic of otherness, is fundamentally ethical. Openness to the other is just such an ethical sensibility and, as we have seen, for Levinas it is first philosophy.

Both Freud and Levinas speak of narcissism, albeit in varying contexts. Freud speaks of the human's "natural narcissism" (16) which is threatened by a natural world, and even a civilization, that does not appear to place human concerns at the fore. Despite this narcissism, humans must overcome it, come to terms with the world's hostility, receive "education to reality," and refuse permanent infantilism. Levinas speaks, in "Philosophy and the Idea of Infinity," of narcissistic philosophy which reduces all things foreign to something familiar, so that all features of otherness fade in order to maintain the security and comfort of the narcissistic ego. His ethical philosophy seeks to correct such philosophical reductions by prioritizing a radical and irreducible Other, an Other who wards off narcissism. I have suggested that nature in the Dillardian religious vision stands as an Other in the spirit of Levinas, an Other that corrects narcissism by illustrating in often graphic and gory terms the relative insignificance of human endeavor. I further suggest that Dillard's conceptions of deity survive the Freudian critique of religion because of this very feature: resistance to narcissism. Such resistance to narcissism refuses to allow the desire for a liberator to override what is amply evident in the natural world, namely, that nature's (and by extension, God's) concerns are not to be confused with human concerns. I argue that Dillard, Levinas, Freud, and Feuerbach, in their respective projects, are invested in exposing and resisting the narcissistic feature in human philosophical and religious constructions. In this way, they stand opposed to those dominant feminist theologies that cling to a measure of narcissism even as they claim to resist anthropocentrism. There is yet one more critique of religion I wish to discuss in relation to the themes of this work; to it I now turn.

The Nietzschean Critique of Religion

Nietzsche's comments on religion range throughout many of his works, including *Genealogy of Morals*, *Twilight of the Idols*, and *The Anti-Christ*. Even the most cursory reading familiarizes the reader with his caustic blasts against Judaism and Christianity for what he sees as their inherent hatred for life, demonizing of natural existence, and underlying nihilism. I will not explicate these critiques here.[5] Instead, I briefly will delve into an aspect of Nietzschean thought from which his critiques of religion could be derivative. I am speaking of his views of tragedy and the role of tragic art, and the aesthetic perspective built upon a tragic vision. He explicates these features of his thought most clearly in *The Birth of Tragedy*; however, there are resonances of the tragic theme throughout his work, especially in *Thus Spake Zarathustra*, *The Will to Power*, and in the religious critiques already mentioned. Here, I will focus upon a handful of readings of Nietzsche's *The Birth of Tragedy* in order to elucidate the gist of what he means when he insists upon the value of a tragic perspective. I will then try to insert this tragic perspective into a seam of my argument, in order to illumine ways in which a Dillardian religious vision is, in its own ways, a tragic one to be distinguished from the more saccharine feminist accounts of human existence in the world.

To say that *The Birth of Tragedy* concerns itself with proposing the Greek god Dionysus as a metaphor for a way of life focusing on ecstatic affirmation of existence and of tragedy is to simplify only mildly. Although Nietzsche does not mention Christianity in *The Birth of Tragedy*, there is a real sense in which Christianity (and/or a traditional western religious perspective) in general stands in the background of what Nietzsche opposes to Dionysus and the life perspective he represents. In *Ecce Homo* Nietzsche comments on his silence about Christianity in *The Birth of Tragedy* and states that Christianity "negates all aesthetic values—the only values recognized in *The Birth of Tragedy*: it is nihilistic in the most profound sense, while in the Dionysian symbol the ultimate limit of affirmation is attained" (271). Christianity, as the culmination of western religious thought *and* as a way of life or worldview, stands in utter opposition to the life perspective symbolized by Dionysus. The difference between the two perspectives has to do with the approach and response each has to tragedy.

Gilles Deleuze states in his *Nietzsche and Philosophy* that Nietzsche

> opposes the tragic vision of the world to two others: the dialectical and the Christian. Or rather, more accurately, tragedy has three ways of dying. It dies a first time by Socrates' dialectic, this is its "Euripidean" death. It dies a second time by Christianity and a third time under the combined blows of the modern dialectic . . . Nietzsche insists upon the fundamentally Christian character of the dialectic and of German philosophy and on the congenital incapacity of Christianity and the dialectic to live, understand or think the tragic. (10–1)

It is their inability to "live, understand or think the tragic" that makes Socrates and Christianity the antitheses of Dionysus. For Nietzsche, the approach one takes to the tragic is a key indication of the value of one's perspective, the value for transforming life. Richard Schacht explains:

> The birth of tragedy for Nietzsche was an event of the greatest significance; for it did not merely involve the appearance of a new art-form, thus opening another chapter in the development of art. It also made possible a further transformation of human life, which he conceives to have been and to be of far greater moment

than is generally recognized. He does not regard tragic art as a phenomenon the significance of which is confined to but a single sphere of human experience and cultural life. Rather, he views it as the potential foundation and guiding force of an entire form of culture and human existence, which alone is capable of filling the void left by the collapse of 'optimistic' life-sustaining myths (both religious and philosophical-scientific). (497)

The tragic, or an aesthetic built upon the tragic, is for Nietzsche a kind of "redemptive strategy"[6] that supplants those optimistic versions offered by philosophy and religion. In the symbol of Dionysus, Nietzsche posits a way by which one authentically confronts the "awfulness or absurdity of existence" and "the terrors of individual existence" (Nietzsche 1910, 62, 128); in short, the tragedy of human life. Moreover, he suggests that in facing such horrific aspects of human existence, one can be transformed and exhilarated. Tragic art, for example, can induce this exhilaration. Nietzsche explains:

> Dionysian art, too, seeks to convince us of the eternal joy of existence: only we are to seek this joy not in phenomena, but behind phenomena. We are to perceive how all that comes into being must be ready for a sorrowful end; we are compelled to look into the terror of existence—yet we are not to become torpid . . . We are really for brief moments Primordial Being itself, and feel its indomitable desire for being and joy in existence; the struggle, the pain, the destruction of phenomena, now appear to us as something necessary . . . We are pierced by the maddening stings of these pains at the very moment when we have become, as it were, one with the immeasurable primordial joy in existence, and when we anticipate, in Dionysian ecstasy, the indestructibility and eternity of this joy. In spite of fear and pity, we are the happy living beings, not as individuals, but as the *one* living being, with whose procreative joy we are blended. (128–9)

I quote at length here because this passage contains references to an important aspect of the tragic vision of which Nietzsche speaks: the flux of all things or the chaos of the cosmos. Deleuze discusses this aspect of Nietzschean thought in a section titled "The Dicethrow" in which he offers a reading of several sections of Nietzsche's *Thus Spake Zarathustra* that speak of reason and chance. Of the several sections, section 48 entitled "Before Sunrise" hints most directly at the chaos, or lack of order, that is at the heart of tragic vision.

In "Before Sunrise," Zarathustra speaks to heaven as if addressing an entity. His speech resembles a prayer of devotion or a love poem, for he speaks of heaven's beauty, his longing for the vision of heaven, and of the unspeakable knowledge he and heaven have of each other, the intimacy of their relations. Zarathustra continually affirms the feature he and heaven have in common: "the vast unbounded Yea- and Amen-saying" (182). He grumbles against those things that would prevent his communion with heaven, that block him from heaven's light; he longs to stand, arms upraised, before the "abyss of light" (183) that symbolizes eternity. He exclaims:

> For all things are baptized at the font of eternity, and beyond good and evil; good and evil themselves, however, are but fugitive shadows and damp afflictions and passing clouds. Verily, it is a blessing and not a blasphemy when I teach that "above all things there standeth the heaven of chance, the heaven of innocence, the heaven of hazard, the heaven of wantonness." (183)

Two of the most despised "passing clouds" which block Zarathustra's communion and Yea-saying are the clouds of reason and order. Reason imposes an order upon the world through philosophical or religious systems, so that all things are categorized as either good or evil, depending upon, usually, whether or not they serve human purposes. At the font of heaven, however, all things—all the terrors of life, the horrific aspects of human existence—become sanctified, "baptized," and are affirmed. Moreover, the font itself, heaven, is seen to be not one of order or reason or Will, but of chance and randomness and flux. Here, Nietzsche's particular brand of antirationalism shows:

> This freedom and celestial serenity did I put like an azure bell above all things, when I taught that over them and through them, no "eternal Will"—willeth. This wantonness and folly did I put in place of that Will, when I taught that "In everything there is one thing impossible—rationality!" A *little* reason, to be sure, a germ of wisdom scattered from star to star—this leaven is mixed in all things: for the sake of folly, wisdom is mixed in all things! A little wisdom is indeed possible; but this blessed security have I found in all things, that they prefer—*to dance* on the feet of chance. O heaven above me! thou pure, thou lofty heaven! This is now thy purity unto me, that there is no eternal reason-spider and reason-cobweb:—That thou art to me a dancing-floor for divine chances, that thou art to me a table of the Gods, for divine dice and dice-players. (183–4)

I will resist the dense and lengthy analysis that this passage deserves in favor of one that gets more to the point of my argument. Here, Nietzsche is affirming the random and chaotic nature of the world over against the rationally ordered and moral versions of the world offered by dominant, Christianized western philosophy and religion. He is affirming a flux of life in which the Dionysian can "dance on the feet of chance," revelling ecstatically in chaotic freedom, unencumbered by the spiders and cobwebs that try to enframe or contain the world's chaos and order it into a rational, manageable, ultimately useful system. This chaos is experienced as terrible by those who cling to the illusions offered by religion and philosophy; it is, however, experienced as joyful and exhilarating by those who have developed to the highest possible state, a state that accommodates the tragic as being what it is, not what one wishes it to be. Schacht explains:

> [Tragic art] works a transformation upon our consciousness of the human reality
> that is also our own, at the same time as it reflects that reality for us to behold. The
> fate of the tragic figure takes on the aspect of something sublime rather than
> merely horrible; and thus, without being denied or glossed over, it ceases to inspire
> mere 'nausea' and moves us instead to fascination and awe . . . Tragic art presents
> us neither with an ideal to be admired and emulated, nor with an avenue by means
> of which to escape all thought of the hard realities of life . . . In short, tragic art
> provides us with a way of apprehending this reality that enables us to come to
> terms with it—and not only to endure but also to affirm what we see, as we thereby
> learn to see it. (500–1)

Through this transformation of human consciousness, the world ceases to be a
place that needs philosophical or religious justification. The world ceases to be a
stumbling block and offense, in need of explaining and ordering in accordance
with human norms of morality and justice. To the contrary, the world is allowed to
be what it is in all its randomness, terror, destruction, and indifference to human
life and, in being such, provokes deep feelings of awe, joy, and exhilaration.

Deleuze expounds upon the dice imagery Nietzsche uses toward the end of
"Before Sunrise," quoted above, and argues that, for Nietzsche, there are two types
of players at the dicetable. "The bad player, " Deleuze explains, "counts on several
throws of the dice, on a great number of throws. In this way he makes use of
causality and probability to produce a combination that he sees as desirable. He
posits this combination itself as an end to be obtained, hidden behind causality"
(26–7). The bad player is like a spider behind a great web, who traps those things
that are free in its net; the bad player intercepts the free play of chance and wrestles
it into a causal scheme to produce desired results. The good player, however, affirms
chance and freedom from the outset and throws the dice only once, allowing the
dice and chance to fatally determine the combination, a combination which the
good player then affirms. It is a combination both "fatal and loved" (27). This
good player is analogous to the Dionysian, to the one of transformed human
consciousness, to the Overman—the one who affirms the flux of all things, does
not shrink from the terrors and pain of existence, and does not feel the need to lay
philosophical or religious grids of illusion upon the world in order to minimize its
horrors and justify it to human moral codes and sensibilities. Such a transformed
human being affirms existence and the world as it is and finds occasion to exult in
that world. Herein lies the importance of the tragic vision for Nietzsche: it allows
one not only to endure the harsh and exacting world, but to affirm it, to see oneself
as part of it, even as one with it.

I suggest that a major difference between the Dillardian religious vision and
that of dominant feminist theologies lies in their respective approaches to the
violence and terror in the natural world. In Nietzschean terms, this difference is
measured by the capacity of each to "live, understand or think the tragic," which
involves being able to affirm the chaos and flux of all things, and to refrain from

passing judgment upon a natural world that does not have human comfort as its ordered and rational telos. By now, the direction of my argument should be clear, namely, that the Dillardian religious vision, as I have explicated it, accommodates a Nietzschean sense of the tragic, while the dominant contemporary feminist theologies maintain a web of illusion through which the tragic is either dulled or ignored in order to achieve desired ideological and political goals. In short, contemporary politico-theological ideologies, including many feminist theologies, typify the perspective of Nietzsche's bad dicethrowers.

There are several examples in Dillard's work that illustrate the transformation of human consciousness and the affirmation of chance that seem central to the Nietzschean sense of the tragic. I mention only two, and they are two that are considered earlier in this work. The first is the mangrove island Dillard writes of in her essay "Sojourner." As stated above, the mangrove island is the archimage of the freedom and beauty that come from yielding to both chance and necessity. It drifts over the alien ocean, pushed by various currents and winds, mindlessly submitting to, and thus affirming, the forces that shape and direct it. Dillard suggests the mangrove as an ideal for human life and consciousness, for we too are thrust into existence on a planet that has itself been thrown into orbit within a galaxy that seems like a campfire ringed with small rocks. Humans, she suggests, could copy the mangroves and live in the often hostile world "exposed . . . beautiful and loose . . . turn[ing] drift into dance" (Dillard 1982b, 152). Rather than fleeing to the comfort zones of a religious system that minimizes or omits the randomness of our existence, Dillard looks for the "possibilities for beauty" (152) in such a vision and, thereby, affirms the tragic aspects of existence in a way that dominant feminist theologies do not.

Clare Fishburn, a character in Dillard's *The Living*, is an example of a human consciousness that undergoes transformation after facing squarely the tragic dimensions of his own life, namely, the eventuality of his death. After managing to survive in the harsh and exacting landscape of Puget Sound, he then has to deal with a death threat made against him by a power-hungry intellectual, Obenchain. Clare lives in fear for a few weeks, looking before turning corners and sleeping with the lights on. Finally, however, his consciousness is transformed by an epiphany of a farmer being plowed into the earth along with his horse and tools. Clare realizes that, whether or not Obenchain carries out his death threat, he is going to die anyway, as will everyone else. Rather than escaping into the illusion of a heavenly existence that would take up where his earthly one leaves off, Clare simply faces the eventuality and finality of his death as a fact of existence in this world. Furthermore, rather than falling into pessimism and melancholy, Clare is afforded a new sense of freedom and throughout the rest of the novel lives in a way that is more authentic, and more fundamentally affirming of the world and his place in it. Clare, I think, is an example of a Yea-sayer, of one who comes to terms with the randomness of life and the sorrows of existence *not* by escaping into a philosophical or religious system that reduces them or organizes them in a way that makes them ultimately serve human goals, but by affirming them *in their reality* and by accepting his place in relation to them. He develops the capacity to "live, understand and think the tragic," which then allows him to affirm the world in all its terror, harshness, and flux. Of course, one may well say that Clare learns this capacity from his mother, Ada, who often shocked people with her sense of the cruelty of God and the tragedy of life. Remember that on her deathbed, she reflects positively on her life which has been marked and scarred by loss and hardship. She concludes that her life has been a good one, for she had "got so deep into the battering and jabbing of it all" and "she took part in the great drama" (334). Ada, too, turns drift into dance and affirms her oneness with and her existence in a world that is costly and racked with sorrows, thus showing her capacity to think and live the tragic. These—mangroves, Clare, and Ada—are only three of many in Dillard's work who live life with a sense of the tragic. These examples, combined with her conception of the menacing and chaotic world in *Pilgrim at Tinker Creek*, illustrate that Dillard's entire religious vision is one that has as its heart an affirmation of the tragic and violent aspects of human existence in the natural world. Indeed, the guiding premise of *Pilgrim* could well be what Silk and Stern claim is the lesson of Greek tragedy for Nietzsche, namely, that "a beautiful surface may conceal terrible depths" (52). This affirmation of tragic existence is what marks the dividing line between her perspective and the dominant feminist religious perspectives in spite of the fact that both claim to have the natural world as the ground of their thought.

The religious vision typified by McFague's work is an affirmation in its own way; it affirms many aspects of human existence that traditional western religion has despised, such as the embodied and sexual dimensions of life. Praiseworthy as such an affirmation is, it comes, however, within a larger religious vision that still sees the need to justify the natural world, or at least certain parts of it. This view extols the natural world as that which should be at the center of a religious perspective in the "ecological, nuclear age" yet omits or refuses to acknowledge the features of the world that do not readily adhere to certain ideological and political goals. In this way, it remains as one of the "optimistic, life-sustaining myths" which, according to Nietzsche, condemn and judge the world in a spirit of bad faith, rather than affirm it as it is, and seek to place a web of reason and moral strictures upon the world so that it serves human ends and operates according to human principles of morality.

Such concern with human interest serves to define the dominant feminist perspective as a fundamentally theological one rather than an aesthetic one. James Hans draws the distinction between the aesthetic and the theological in his book *The Origin of the Gods*. He explains that "both the theological and the aesthetic provide descriptions of what is, and both of them articulate a sense of pattern, but the theological always has human interest written into it from the beginning" (26). The world is personalized and humanized in the sense that all things work ultimately to serve a human end. The aesthetic perspective, however, because it is rooted in a Nietzschean sense of the tragic and acknowledgement of the free play of the world, does not make such demands upon the world, especially the natural world. Hans explains:

> If we begin with an aesthetic world, however, this kind of personalization and humanization of the world is no longer necessary [or possible] . . . the aesthetic opens humans up to the nonhuman in the world, and to the nonhuman in themselves; it situates them within the impersonal flows that determine the course of all living matter without judging those flows in terms of their equity or purpose, for they can be said to have no purpose within the aesthetic. The flows flow, and we are part of their flow, but there is nothing to be said beyond that. They do not flow *for* us, they don't lead *to* us; we are simply part of them, like it or not. (26–7, parenthetical content mine)

Granted, the dominant feminist perspective typified by McFague has gone a long way to undercut the ways in which traditional theology has placed human life and concerns at the center of the universe's agenda. Removing the human from the pedestal is the major concern behind McFague's insistence upon the interdependence and interrelation of all things. It is just this tenacious belief, however—the belief that the earth revolves around the human—that sneaks back into the feminist perspective when models of deity are proposed, allegedly rooted in the natural world, that ultimately serve human purposes. As Hans states,

> We have grown to the point where we can concede that the world is *not* something over which we have dominion . . . But we have been so far unwilling to follow through on this fact and recognize that as a consequence we must accept the world's indifference to our presence in it. It could even be said that we have failed to address the problems inherent in our way of life because we still tacitly assume that the earth—like the God who swore after the last major flood that He would never destroy everything again—*does* take our interests and our presence into account. We simply can't seem to get past the notion that it is totally indifferent to us, and until we arrive at that point, we cannot discern the ways in which the aesthetic is that which is left once we strip from the world the meanings we have imposed upon it out of the force of our desire. (29–30)

The desire for a deity who cares about the struggles, rights, and concerns of women and other marginalized groups has overridden the sensibility that, while present in dominant feminist religious thought, is ultimately eclipsed, namely, that the natural world does not exist to serve human goals and neither does any deity modelled upon it. This eclipse insures that the dominant feminist perspective remains a fundamentally theological one, a negative identification in Nietzschean thought. Furthermore, this eclipse shows a great deal of contempory theological revisions to be less than revisionary, in that they retain the fundamental philosophical assumptions of the racist, sexist, hegemonic, etc. theological systems they claim to revise. The Dillardian vision, because it forces one to stare directly into the glare of the world's indifference to human endeavors, incorporates a Nietzschean sense of the tragic and qualifies as an aesthetic perspective. Dillard's approach is an aesthetic one on her own terms already in that her methodology, while appropriating various philosophical and theological traditions, is comprised primarily in her stated effort to read the raw, natural world as a text and to let it tell her what it means. Such a hermeneutical stance is one that sees the text (here, nature) as an Other, rather than imposing upon the text predetermined meanings and justifications.

The dominant feminist perspective, while an affirmation of sorts, fails to incorporate the tragic dimension of human existence in the natural world, as evidenced by the docility and benevolence of the models of deity it derives from that world. Rather than affirming the world, those of this perspective arrange the natural world like flowers on a coffee table in order to affirm and advance their own political, social, and economic goals. The world and the deity modelled upon it, then, become domestic servants. Nietzsche rails at the offensiveness of such an idea, claiming that "God as a domestic servant, as a postman, as an almanac-maker . . . is so absurd a God he would have to be abolished even if he existed" (Nietzsche 1968, 170). As the epigraph to this chapter asserts, such an egoistic conception of deity is the very thing that "religious faith requires us to renounce." Such a renunciation, I hope I have shown, is at the heart of the Dillardian religious vision and, thus, shows its compatibility with important aspects of the Feuerbachian, Freudian, and Nietzschean critiques of religion.

Notes

1. McFague acknowledges that human well-being is not maintained in the universe at any price. Some species have to die in order for others to live—this is a reality in her vision of the world that emphasizes radical interdependence and is not anthropocentric. She, however, does not seem to appreciate the way in which such an acknowledgement fundamentally undermines her whole theological/ideological edifice.

2. I use *The Future of an Illusion* despite Tomoko Masuzawa's recent revisionist argument that *Totem and Taboo* is the most important text of Freud's concerning religion. See pp. 78, 194 n. 9. Granted, there is a curious avoidance of the parricide in *Totem and Taboo* by scholars in religion. I avoid it here not because of its scandal, but because of its irrelevance to the issues in this work, namely, the development of certain constructions of deity, the role of nature in these developments, and the importance of consolation in religious systems. *The Future of an Illusion* speaks to these concerns directly. Whatever reservations Freud had about the book cannot undermine the effect it has had on religious inquiry.

3. Preus explains that religion is a prized asset of civilization because of "its effectiveness at being both compensatory and repressive . . . As repression, religion threatens punishment; as compensation, it promises divine protection, consolation, and recompense against all the engines of suffering" (192).

4. Philip Rieff notes the open hostility that Freud exhibits toward religion in general and, especially, to philosophers of religion "who try to make religion intellectually, as well as emotionally, attractive" (263).

5. One might make an interesting argument in which the pale, sickly spider deity Nietzsche excoriates in *The Anti-Christ* (127–8) is seen as analogous to the domesticated and reduced deity of some liberation theologians. Nietzsche's comments on the decay of God (128) and the Christian drive to domesticate (131–2) would be pertinent in such an argument and would serve me. Instead of this line of thinking, however, I focus here upon Nietzsche's view of tragedy and the implications this has for religion. In this way, the larger significance of his thought is taken into account.

6. I borrow this term from Robert E. McGinn, "Culture as Prophylactic: Nietzsche's *Birth of Tragedy* as Culture Criticism," *Nietzsche-Studien* 4 (1975):75–138.

Conclusion

Violent models of God have been used for centuries as ideological weapons of oppression. Certainly the great western monotheisms of Judaism, Christianity, and Islam have wielded mighty representations of God as conqueror, warrior, and victor, among others, in order to justify wars, expand empires, conquer rival viewpoints and keep whole races, genders, and ethnicities in bondage of some form or another. Why, then, given such a horrific history, would anyone advocate reclaiming violent images of deity? And if such a reclaiming can be defended, how can violent models be reclaimed without them undergirding, once again, all manner of oppressive ideologies and actions?

The answer to the first question, I hope, is obvious by now. Violent models of deity are a logical outgrowth of any theology that seeks to ground its understanding of God in the natural world. Any honest look at the natural world must acknowledge its paradoxically beautiful and terrifying violence; therefore, the deity modelled upon it must bear those same qualities. Given this, perhaps a better question is, Why model God upon the natural world? Of course, Platonists, Neoplatonists and transcendentalists have their reasons, reasons tied closely to their understanding of the world as an emanation from God, as the lively material 'shadow' of the infinitely non-material Spirit or Mind that creates and sustains all things. For those outside such philosophical and/or theological traditions, however, there still remains a powerful reason for using the natural world as a model for God. The reason is this: humans did not create it. The natural world is not the work of human invention and, therefore, it can serve more legitimately than anything or anyone else as a ground for characterizing God without automatically falling prey to the criticisms of Feuerbach, Freud, and Nietzsche. This holds despite the fact that even in our clearest moments, we see and know only our perceptions of the world, and not the world in itself. Our perceptions change, our science changes—everything changes—but this does not undermine the fact that the natural world, correctly understood or not, is the most stable and consistent aspect of our reality. It *is* our reality, whether or not we like it or know it. And nature is violent.

How can violent models of God be reclaimed without them once again undergirding oppression? My answer to this is highly involved and requires more space than I can give it here; however, a few comments can illumine the basic direction my thinking takes on this issue. Ultimately, the answer to this question forces us to critically analyze the extent to which God can or cannot be used to undergird *any ideology at all*, oppressive or not. Let me explain.

Since the Enlightenment and the rise of the scientific worldview, theologians of all stripes have been faced with enormous intellectual challenges, not least of which is how to ground the claims of faith on something other than faith. Moreover, theologians are faced with the task of defending faith claims against critics like Feuerbach, Freud, and Nietzsche who view them as manifestations of various projections, wish fulfillments, and revengeful wills to power. Luther's famous Reformation claim of *sola fide* functions well within an intellectual milieu that still sees theology as the queen of the sciences. We in the twenty-first century, however, no longer live in such an age; indeed, we are removed by such an age by over three centuries. Religious worldviews must transform and translate themselves into the modern and postmodern climate if they are to be anything other than alternative, parallel conceptual universes out of touch with the larger intellectual culture. After all, on the basis of sheer faith, one can believe *anything* without regard for its resonance with larger human experience or knowledge. After taking a leap of faith, all sorts of deities, realities, actions, and claims are possible. The United States, with its expansive, richly diverse and creative religious landscape, is a testament to what faith can create when given free range of motion.

Political theologians, like McFague and others, face particularly difficult intellectual challenges quite apart from the most obvious obstacle posed by the fact that the unjust belief systems and practices they align themselves against are some of the most longstanding and deeply entrenched on the planet. Political theologians—by virtue of being both *political* and *theologians*—take on the task of formulating theology in a way that compels certain political actions, and advances particular ideological agendas. Political theologians put their political agenda "front and center" and then revise theology—including models of God, the divine/world relation, human/human relations—in ways that are to ground and advance their political aim, not only among themselves but in larger society. Such theologies fail, however, along with all other theologies—political or otherwise—if their ground is rooted solely in faith. Claims or calls for action rooted in faith alone—no matter how desirable—are not a stable ground for political action in the contemporary world. The claims of any effective political action must be rooted in something other than gods, realities, or worlds that themselves are grounded only in faith. Why? Because faith claims cannot be proven or disproven, and therefore faith in them cannot be compelled or "expected" in others who have not taken the leap. Furthermore, as has been discussed above, the gods, worlds, and realities claimed by faith are often nothing more than veiled projections, wish fulfillments, and delusion. To have any chance at legitimately appealing to larger audiences outside the faith, and to have any broad, effective role in political change, faith claims must be consistent or resonant with other, more provable, received or agreed-upon principles, documents or beliefs. Martin Luther King, Jr., for example, knew this when he wrote his powerful letter from the jail cell in Birmingham. Toward the end of the letter, he grounds his hope for just civil rights legislation on two distinctly different platforms. First, he grounds his call in the Christian vision, rooted solely in faith in a just God who created all people in his image, and in a sacred text that testifies to such. Secondly, he bases his call in the more secular American vision, rooted in broad Enlightenment claims about liberty, equality, and human dignity, and in a Constitution and Bill of Rights that legally upholds those claims. King's position is intellectually powerful here because he casts his net as broadly as possible, aiming his argument not only at Christians who share his faith commitments, but also at *non-religious Americans*, or indeed *anyone* who adheres to the broad political, social, and ethical maxims that have dominated western polity for the last three hundred years. King knew that his call for action, while deeply rooted in his own Christian faith, had to reach beyond the limitations of his personal "faith world" and appeal to those vast numbers of people who would forever be outside the faith community, but who nevertheless shared some of its convictions albeit on different grounds. Any political theology that seeks to affect larger culture must face the limitations of being a *theology*—that is, something rooted in faith which obtains only to those who have taken the leap—and must adjust itself accordingly. Add to this task the important step of surviving the critiques of religion discussed earlier.

McFague takes an important step toward making her brand of political theology tenable to those outside a "faith world" when she attempts to ground her models of God in nature, or the universe. The universe is, after all, the ground and condition of all known existence, human or otherwise. Rather than relying on ancient scriptural claims or outdated theological arguments to define the God of her theology, McFague tries valiantly to revise and transform God in a way consistent with contemporary scientific theories of the universe and the common fund of human experience in the natural world. Other liberationist, environmentalist, feminist, and process theologians hold hands with McFague here despite, perhaps, disagreeing with other specific features of her theology. For every step she makes, however, toward grounding her theology in broadly scientific, empirical claims—claims that will hold in an evolutionary and nuclear age—she reaffirms one particular faith claim that serves as the Achilles' heel of her entire theological edifice, insofar as it seeks to cohere with a larger contemporary and scientific worldview. She takes as a given—on the basis of sheer faith—that "the universe is neither indifferent or malevolent but that there is a power (and a personal power at that) which is on the side of life and its fulfillment . . ." (McFeague 1987, x). The universe is, or contains, or is synonymous with a personal power that sides with life and its fulfillment. This is an important claim for McFague—and indeed for any number of contemporary political theologians—because it is this claim which allows her to argue ultimately that God as Lover, Mother, and Friend is a personal cosmic power who is "on the side of" women and other marginalized groups in their fight for "life" and "fulfillment," which usually translates for McFague and others into very specific positions on issues relevant to women, ranging from abortion rights to lesbian healthcare benefits. In short, the universe takes women's side in the fight for social justice.

Well, this is unacceptable and cannot count as theology for an evolutionary and nuclear age. First of all, this theology assumes *a priori* the existence of a cosmic, personal power that is benevolent and just in the ways humans commonly define these terms. No scholar living after Hume can make such a claim without doing much more heavy lifting than McFague does in order to justify it. Secondly, the radical dissonance between this benevolent, just, and personal cosmic power (God), on the one hand, and the actual, observable universe that allegedly mirrors this God, on the other, exposes McFague's "evolutionary, nuclear" theology for what it is: a great wish for the universe and the God in it to be other than they are with regard to the plight of specific individuals. One does not have to read the entire corpus of a nature writer like Dillard to see that McFague's cosmic God has gotten a makeover once abstracted from his/her ground in the universe. Even the most cursory glance at the Discovery Channel illumines a universe vast and magnificent, both terrifying and thrilling, that while certainly sustaining humans as a species, has no apparent *personal* concern for the individuals of any particular species, marginalized or not. McFague is right to attempt to ground theology in nature. Natural theology—that is, a theology whose images of deity are derived from nature—is perhaps the only kind of theology that can escape the powerful challenges of Feuerbach and others. Nature is given; it predates human existence. We are not its creator or author; it is not made in our image or with our individual, specific interests in mind. This being the case, any theology rooted in an honest understanding of it can escape the charges of being a system of denial and consolation, delusional wish fulfillment, or a mechanism designed to exact eternal revenge on its enemies by aligning the entire cosmic order according to its whims. Such a natural theology, however, must be *honest*, and ever-vigilant against the temptation either to ascribe to nature traits and characteristics that are foreign to it, or to excise from it features—like violence and indifference to suffering—that do not suit our desires or political agendas. To reclaim violent models of God is simply to be honest about the universe we live in and the cosmic, natural powers that seem to "brood and light" within it. And as we have seen, these powers *cannot* be represented accurately as mother, lover, and friend.

So, perhaps the most important question concerns not so much how oppressive ideologies can be kept from using violent models of God. The more important question is: can God—violent or not—be used to support any ideology at all, oppressive or not? Can the God modelled upon nature be said to support any political ideology? No. Nature and the deity abstracted from it are both indifferent to political ideologies of all stripes. So, oppressive ideologies that use violent models of God to undergird the violent regimes that proceed from them are intellectually flawed and illegitimate. Equally as flawed are the non-oppressive ideologies, including the political theologies of McFague and others, that try to align God with politically indifferent nature and with highly politicized ideologies at the same time. No ideology or theology can legitimately claim a nature deity, or a deity whose character is aligned closely with nature, as its proponent. Nature doesn't do politics.

Natural theology, as I have discussed it here, means the end of political theology, at least intellectually. Of course, those with ideologies to wield and worlds to remake are not usually so easily deterred by such details. Those who wish to use God as the poster-deity for their political platform will continue to do so, if for no other reason than doing so often is highly successful, even in the so-called "scientific" western world. And so the debates will rage on, each group aligned against its enemies, all of them holding banners and wearing their respective T-shirts, all claiming that God is on their side and denouncing the opposing group for daring to think that God would be on *their* side. Regularly and without fail, however, nature will rise up and kill a random number of people—perhaps an entire town or country even—with a strong wind, a rising tide, or an invisible virus. In those moments we see truly whose side the power of the universe is on: its own.

Works Cited

Albanese, Catherine. 1988. Transcendentalism. *Encyclopedia of American Religious Experience: Studies of Traditions and Movements*. Edited by Charles H. Lippy and Peter W. Williams. Vol. 2. New York: Charles Scribner's Sons.

—————. 1990. *Nature Religion in America: From the Algonkian Indians to the New Age*. Chicago: University of Chicago Press.

Armstrong, A. Hilary. 1979. 'Emanation' in Plotinus. In *Plotinian and Christian Studies*. London: Variorum Reprints.

Bernasconi, Robert. 1988. The Trace of Levinas in Derrida. In *Derrida and Differance*. Edited by David Wood and Robert Bernasconi. Evanston: Northwestern University Press.

Brehier, Emile. 1958. *The Philosophy of Plotinus*. Translated by Joseph Thomas. Chicago: University of Chicago Press.

Brown, Stuart Gregory. 1945. Emerson's Platonism. *The New England Quarterly* 18:325–45.

Bultmann, Rudolf. 1961. *Kerygma and Myth: A Theological Debate*, with Ernst Lohmeyer, Julius Schniewind, Helmut Thielicke, and Austin Farrer. Edited by Hans Werner Bartsch and translated by Reginald H. Fuller. New York: Harper and Row.

Cantwell, Mary. 1992. A Pilgrim's Progress. *New York Times Magazine* 26 (April): 34–42.

Cherry, Conrad. 1980. *Nature and Religious Imagination: From Edwards to Bushnell*. Philadelphia: Fortress Press.

Cohen, Richard A., ed. 1986. *Face to Face with Levinas*. New York: State University of New York Press.

Deleuze, Gilles. 1983. *Nietzsche and Philosophy*. Translated by Hugh Tomlinson. New York: Columbia University Press.

Derrida, Jacques. 1978. Violence and Metaphysics: An Essay on the Thought of Emmanuel Levinas. In *Writing and Difference*. Translated by Alan Bass. Chicago: University of Chicago Press.

—————. 1981. *Dissemination*. Translated by Barbara Johnson. Chicago: University of Chicago Press.

Dillard, Annie. 1974. *Pilgrim at Tinker Creek*. New York: Harper and Row.

—————. 1977. *Holy the Firm*. New York: Harper and Row.

—————. 1982a. *Living by Fiction*. New York: Harper and Row.

—————. 1982b. *Teaching a Stone to Talk: Expeditions and Encounters*. Harper and Row.

—————. 1991. *The Living*. New York: Harper and Row.

Edwards, Jonathan. 1948. *Images or Shadows of Divine Things*. Edited by Perry Miller. New Haven: Yale University Press.

Feuerbach, Ludwig. 1957. *The Essence of Christianity*. Edited by E. Graham Waring and F.W. Strothmann. New York: Frederick Unger Publishing Company.

—————. 1967. *Lectures on the Essence of Religion*. Translated by Ralph Manheim. New York: Harper and Row.

Fitzgerald, Karen. 1985. The Good Books: Writers' Choices. *Ms. Magazine* 14 (December): 80.

Freud, Sigmund. 1975. *The Future of an Illusion*. Translated by James Strachey. New York: W.W. Norton and Company.

Fritzell, Peter. 1990. *Nature Writing and America: Essays Upon a Cultural Type*. Ames: Iowa State University Press.

Gay, Peter. 1987. *A Godless Jew: Freud, Atheism, and the Making of Psychoanalysis*. New Haven: Yale University Press.

Goldman, Stan. 1991. Sacrifices to the Hidden God: Annie Dillard's *Pilgrim at Tinker Creek* and Leviticus. *Soundings* V74 (Spring/Summer): 195–213.

Gura, Philip F. 1981. *The Wisdom of Words: Language, Theology and Literature in the New England Renaissance*. Middletown: Wesleyan University Press.

Gustafson, James M. 1981 and 1984. *Ethics from a Theocentric Perspective*. 2 vols. Chicago: University of Chicago Press.

Hans, James S. 1991. *The Origin of the Gods*. Albany: State University of New York Press.

Holbrook, Clyde A. 1953. Jonathan Edwards and His Detractors. *Theology Today* 10 (October): 384–97.

Jeffreys, M. V. C. 1967. *John Locke: Prophet of Common Sense*. London: Methuen and Company.

Kamenka, Eugene. 1970. *The Philosophy of Ludwig Feuerbach*. London: Routledge and Kegan Paul.

Kearney, Richard, ed. 1989. Jacques Derrida. In *Dialogues with Contemporary Continental Thinkers*. Chicago: University of Chicago Press.

Lasch, Christopher. 1991. The Illusion of Disillusionment. *Harpers* 283 (July): 19–22.

Levinas, Emmanuel. 1969. *Totality and Infinity: An Essay on Exteriority*. Translated by Alphonso Lingis. Pittsburgh: Duquesne University Press.

——————. 1978. *Existence and Existents*. Translated by Alphonso Lingis. The Hague: Martinus Nijhoff Publishers.

——————. 1981. *Otherwise than Being or Beyond Essence*. Translated by Alphonso Lingis. The Hague: Martinus Nijhoff Publishers.

——————. 1986. The Trace of the Other. In *Deconstruction in Context: Literature and Philosophy*. Edited by Mark C. Taylor. Chicago: University of Chicago Press.

——————. 1987a. Philosophy and the Idea of the Infinite. In *Collected Philosophical Papers*. Translated by Alphonso Lingis. Dordrecht: Martinus Nijhoff Publishers.

——————. 1987b. Meaning and Sense. In *Collected Philosophical Papers*. Translated by Alphonso Lingis. Dordrecht: Martinus Nijhoff Publishers.

——————. 1987c. *Time and the Other [and additional essays]*. Translated by Richard A. Cohen. Pittsburgh: Duquesne University Press.

Locke, John. 1850. *An Essay Concerning Human Understanding and A Treatise on the Conduct of Understanding*. Philadelphia: Troutman and Hayes.

Marion, Jean-Luc. 1991. *God Without Being*. Translated by Thomas A. Carlson. Chicago: University of Chicago Press.

Masuzawa, Tomoko. 1993. *In Search of Dreamtime: The Quest for the Origins of Religion*. Chicago: University of Chicago Press.

McFague, Sallie. 1987. *Models of God: Theology for an Ecological, Nuclear Age*. Philadelphia: Fortress.

——————. 1993. *The Body of God: An Ecological Theology*. Minneapolis: Fortress.

McGuinn, Robert E. 1975. Culture as Prophylactic: Nietzsche's *Birth of Tragedy* as Culture Criticism. *Nietzsche-Studien* Vol. 4:75–138.

McIlroy, Gary. 1987. *Pilgrim at Tinker Creek* and the Burden of Science. *American Literature* 59 (March): 71–84.

Miller, Perry. 1964. *Errand into the Wilderness*. New York: Harper and Row.

Moore, Stephen D. 1989. *Literary Criticism and the Gospels: The Theoretical Challenge*. New Haven: Yale University Press.

Moritz, Charles, ed. 1983. Annie Dillard. In *Current Biography Yearbook*. New York: H.W. Wilson Company.

Nietzsche, Friedrich. 1910. *The Birth of Tragedy*. Translated by William A. Haussmann. In *The Complete Works of Friedrich Nietzsche*. Edited by Oscar Levy. London: T. N. Foulis.

——————. 1964. *Thus Spake Zarathustra*. Translated by Thomas Common. New York: Modern Library.

——————. 1967. *On the Genealogy of Morals/Ecce Homo*. Translated by Walter Kaufmann and R. J. Hollingdale. New York: Vintage Books.

——————. 1968. *Twilight of the Idols/The Anti-Christ*. Translated by R. J. Hollingdale. New York: Penguin Books.

Paul, Sherman. 1965. *Emerson's Angle of Vision: Man and Nature in American Experience*. Cambridge: Harvard University Press.

Plato. 1985. *Meno*. Translated and edited by R.W. Sharples. Chicago: Bolchazy-Carducci Publishers.

Preus, J. Samuel. 1987. *Explaining Religion: Criticism and Theory from Bodin to Freud*. New Haven: Yale University Press.

Reed, Sampson. 1970. *Observations on the Growth of the Mind with Remarks on Some Other Subjects*. Introduction by Carl F. Strauch. Gainesville, Fla.: Scholars' Facsimiles and Reprints.

Rieff, Philip. 1959. *Freud: The Mind of the Moralist*. New York: Viking Press.

Schacht, Richard. 1983. *Nietzsche*. London: Routledge and Kegan Paul.

Silk, M. S. and J. P. Stern. 1980. *Nietzsche on Tragedy*. New York: Cambridge University Press.

Smith, Linda. 1991. *Annie Dillard*. New York: Twayne Publishers.

Smithline, Arnold. 1966. *Natural Religion in American Literature*. New Haven: Yale University Press.

Taylor, Mark C. 1993. *Nots*. Chicago: University of Chicago Press.

Wartofsky, Marx W. 1977. *Feuerbach*. New York: Cambridge University Press.

Weil, Simone. 1951. Reflections on the Right Use of School Studies with a View to the Love of God. In *Waiting for God*. Translated by Emma Crawford. New York: G. P. Putnam's Sons.

Wyschogrod, Edith, ed. 1973. Sport, Death and the Elemental. In *The Phenomenon of Death: Faces of Mortality*. New York: Harper Colophon Books.

—————. 1974. *Emmanuel Levinas: The Problem of Ethical Metaphysics*. The Hague: Martinus Nijhoff Publishers.

—————. 1989. Derrida, Levinas, and Violence. In *Derrida and Deconstruction*. Edited by Hugh J. Silverman. New York: Routledge.

Index

About the Author

B. Jill Carroll earned a doctorate in religious studies from Rice University in 1994. She still lives in Houston,Texas, and is currently a lecturer in humanities at Rice. She also serves as an adjunct lecturer in general humanities and religious studies within the University of Houston system.